A Season of Grief

A Season of Grief

a comforting companion for difficult days

Ann Dawson

ave maria press   Notre Dame, Indiana

www.avemariapress.com

International Standard Book Number: 0-87793-978-0

Cover and text design by Brian C. Conley

Printed and bound in the United States of America.

Library of Congress Cataloging-in-Publication Data
Dawson, Ann, 1951-
A season of grief : a comforting companion for difficult days / Ann Dawson.
     p. cm.
Includes bibliographical references.
ISBN 0-87793-978-0 (pbk.)
   1. Consolation. 2. Bereavement--Religious aspects--Christianity.
I. Title.
  BV4905.3 .D38 2002
242'.4--dc21

                         2002004260
                           CIP

Contents

In Memory of Andy
April 7, 1979 - July 27, 1997

Preface

There were once times when I wondered how I would conduct myself in the face of great tragedy. I was certain beyond a doubt that if I should ever have to endure the death of one of my children I would descend, screaming, into insanity. On July 27, 1997, the morning of my husband's forty-seventh birthday, I was to find out just how I would behave. In the early dawn hours of that day, Pat and I sat in a small, cramped office across from a weary young doctor who mumbled the words that mothers hear in their nightmares, words every mother or father fears most. Our eighteen-year-old son, Andrew, the third of our four children, had not survived the injuries he'd sustained in a car accident the week before. Sometime during those early morning hours, he had softly slipped the bonds of this earth. As I sat in that small room, down the hall from where my son's body lay, I did not scream or shout, tear my hair out, or go mad. I simply sat quietly as tears from a well of sorrow so deep within my soul spilled across my face and washed over my heart.

I walked calmly down that hall and into my son's room. I took his hand and laid my head on his chest. I grieved not only for the loss of my son, but also for the part of my own self that had died with him. The world I knew up until that time ended on the day of his death. "I won't survive this," I whispered to my family. "You will," they replied. "We need you." "How can I bear this?" I asked my doctor. "Take these pills," he answered. "Who can get me through this?" I asked my priest. "Prayer" was his reply. "How will I manage?" I asked my friends. They had no answers for me, but they held me up when I would have stumbled.

I was thrown into a fog of grief and despair so thick I thought for a long time that I wouldn't survive the pain. No one seemed to be able to help me make my way through that jungle of grief. I felt completely alone, and in my efforts to find a way across to the other side, back to a "normal" life, I began reading every book I could find that

I thought might give me some insight as to how to survive this awful journey. I began reading books on grief, death and dying, the meaning of suffering, and eternal life. During the course of my reading, I found myself more often than not reaching for a highlighter pen to underline a passage here or there that had made an impact on me. Before I knew it, I had underlined hundreds of quotes from scores of books.

Not long after the funeral, my sister Jill laid a blank journal on my desk. "Now you'll write," she told me. Many weeks later I picked up a pen and opened the booklet to the first blank page. I wrote two words: "Andy died." For long moments, I could do nothing more than stare in disbelief at the horrible words I had written. And then the floodgates opened. I began to fill page after page with my thoughts and feelings. I filled diary pages. I wrote letters and poems. I started contributing to a column for our local newspaper. Many of the topics in that column dealt with handling the death of my child.

Gradually, over a period of time, I began to realize that there should be a way to share with other bereaved people the wealth of quotes that I had collected, quotes that had given me some measure of comfort. The result is this book, a collection not only of quotes but also my own reflections.

Reverend Simon Stephens, founder of The Compassionate Friends, once wrote, "Those of us who have worked through our grief—and found there is a future—are the ones who must meet others in the valley of darkness and bring them to light."

It is my hope that in some small way my words might be able to open a window and let at least a small beacon of light shine upon the darkness of another's grief.

Introduction

And you would accept the seasons of your heart, even as you have always accepted the seasons that pass over your fields. And you would watch with serenity through the winters of your grief.

—KAHLIL GIBRAN, *THE PROPHET*

One of the most difficult discoveries I made early in my "season of grief" was that grief itself has no timetable. I had always managed to face an unpleasant task by reminding myself that by "such and such" date, the ordeal would be over. Before the death of my son I suppose I had foolishly assumed that a period of mourning had a definite course: a beginning, a healing, a recovery, and a return to normalcy. When I encountered people who had been grieving a loss longer than I would have expected, I often found myself feeling almost annoyed with them, thinking that they were malingering, enjoying their state of grief.

But when Andy died, and my world turned upside down, I was terrified at the intensity of the pain. One of the first questions I asked Karen, my grief counselor, was how long this painful period would last. Her response dismayed me because she had no answer. Grief is not a disease of which one is eventually healed. I remember sitting on my front porch not long after Andy's funeral. The pain I felt was such a foreign emotion, such an invader in my life, and I had been struggling so hard to overcome it, to make it disappear. That afternoon as I sat on the porch with my head buried in my hands and tears streaming down my face, I remembered words of a well-known passage from Ecclesiastes: "For everything there is a season, and a time for every matter under heaven: a time to be born, and a time to die . . . a time to weep, and a time to laugh; a time to mourn, and a time to dance . . ." (3:1-2, 4, NRSV). And a little voice in my head whispered, "This is my time to mourn." With that thought, I felt a sense of liberation. I realized that I didn't have to run from the pain. I didn't have to fight it or overcome it. This sorrow, this time of mourning, was a season of my life. All I needed to do was to experience it, to lean into the pain, and to let it become a part of who I was.

We often believe that happiness is a state we should expect and strive for at all times. We look upon sorrow as an unnatural state, and we feel a need to take whatever measures are necessary to restore ourselves to the level of happiness we seek. We waste a lot of time in our grief work when we try to find quick ways to get over the pain. Some people try to escape the pain in ways that are destructive, through drinking or drugs. Others try to escape into a different lifestyle, running as far as they can from old ways that are now associated with the pain of loss. While the majority of us don't become self-destructive, we still fight against this experience of sorrow. I realized that this is an error in our way of thinking. It's okay to be sorrowful, to mourn, to grieve. Indeed, it's not only okay, it is necessary to our spiritual growth.

When I was faced with this realization that day on my front porch and I understood that this was my season of grief, I gave up the struggle and felt a soft peace come over me. This was a part of my life journey, one I needed to experience to the fullest. When I allowed mourning into my life, it became less frightening, not quite a friend, but no longer an alien stranger. I was able to be at peace with my sorrow.

During my own season of grief, I began reading anything I could get my hands on that might help me come to terms with my loss. As I mentioned earlier, I often reached for a highlighter pen to mark certain passages that were especially meaningful to me. When these quotes began to number in the hundreds, I decided to store them on a file in my computer. Gradually, for a reason I couldn't understand at the time, I started adding my own reflections to some of the quotes. Many times, when someone I knew had suffered the loss of a loved one, I delved into my files to try to find words that I might share with them, hoping these passages might be able to give them some measure of the solace I had received from them. The result of those early efforts is this book.

For purposes of reading, I have divided *A Season of Grief* into four parts. These, I believe, are the general emotions we experience during our season of grief: "Time of Loss," "Time of Longing," "Time of Hope," and "Time of Renewal."

The "Time of Loss" is the time of our most intense feeling of bereavement. This is the period we encounter immediately upon the death of the beloved. We are consumed with our feelings of grief and loss. Our feelings overwhelm and incapacitate us. We are undone by our grief and there is a pervading feeling of hopelessness. We are physically impaired by our grief. We can't eat or sleep, and there are moments when we are sure that we will never enjoy any of life's pleasures again. This is a time of questioning old beliefs. We often feel abandoned by God and we are angry with him. Things that were once important to us have become irrelevant in the face of this all-consuming grief.

The "Time of Longing" is less intense than the "Time of Loss." The initial shock has worn off somewhat, but we are cloaked in sorrow. We experience a sense of longing for the beloved. We accept the fact of his or her death, but we desperately miss that person. We are able to function a little more efficiently than in the early days of bereavement, but our thoughts turn again and again to memories of the past. Each anniversary, each holiday is an ordeal. Every day is an effort in coping and coming to terms with our grief. In my experience, during this time of longing, we begin to look for signs of God's presence. We call out for help, and often we are filled with amazement when we begin to realize how near God really is to us. During this time we may enter into a more intimate relationship with God, and we seek a new understanding of things spiritual.

At different times in our season of grief, we will experience a "Time of Hope." This is a time that will overlap all the others. It is the time when our faith rewards us, the season in which we understand that the beloved has not truly left us, but remains always with us in spirit. It is a time of hope because it is during this time that we are comforted in the belief of our eventual reunion. This time of hope is the period in our grief journey when we are given the strength to come to terms with our loss, to incorporate it into our lives, and to live as hope-filled and faith-filled people.

And finally, we experience a "Time of Renewal," a period when grief has softened around us. It is no longer a frightening alien in our lives. We realize that our loved ones have not ceased to exist, but have instead entered into the fullest kind of life, and we are able to rejoice for them in spite of our own feelings of bereavement. We know without a doubt that our loved ones are beside us in a very real, spiritual way. We are able to acknowledge our loss and to integrate it into our being. We are able to say, "I am a widow/an orphan/a parent whose child has died," and rather than being undone by the idea, we are able to integrate it into our new concept of self. We are ready to move forward in our life knowing that death has no power over us.

As anyone who is experiencing a season of grief will know only too well, there is no linear progression through this period. We do not live out a season of grief as we do the seasons we find in nature in an orderly manner, with spring following winter and summer following spring. There will be days very early in our grief that find us experiencing a wonderful sense of "renewal," just as there will occasionally be times many years down the road when we find ourselves reentering the time of "loss." By the same token, this book does not need to be read in any particular order. One day you may feel that you are experiencing a time of "loss" and will turn to the readings in that section. Another time, you might feel that you are in a time of renewal. Hopefully the readings in each section will have some meaning and comfort for you as you progress through your season of grief, and you will begin to understand that even in the darkest days of grief, you are still a beloved child of God who has not been abandoned. It's my intention that each of these readings will serve in some way to reassure you that you will never be alone, that you will always be in the presence of the God who yearns for you to be comforted in your time of sorrow.

One thing that I have learned from entering my own season of grief is that this can be a time of great blessing and growth. It is a time of connection with that which is sacred in life, of communion with the Divine, a time of spiritual awakening. It is my hope that the following pages will help you get in touch with the sacredness within your own wounded spirit.

Time of Loss

> There should be no fear of death, for the death
> of the body is but a gentle passing to a much
> freer life.

—HELEN GREAVES, *TESTIMONY OF LIGHT*

The moment of Andy's actual passing was remarkable only for its uneventfulness. Pat and I were sleeping a few floors above him in a guest wing of the hospital when our phone rang at 5:00 a.m. The nurse told us that the doctor needed to talk to us. I don't remember getting dressed, but I'll never forget the long walk down the hall to the ICU wing. Pat and I held hands, and Pat muttered, "This isn't going to be good" as if to prepare me. I had never been so filled with dread in all my life. The doctor sat us down in a little room and explained to us that a few hours before they had determined that there were signs of brain death. Andy was gone. As simple as that. I had had no maternal premonitions at the moment of his death. He didn't appear to me in a vision to say goodbye. It was just over. The event that shattered my life had happened quietly and with no drama.

I spent the next several hours at Andy's bedside. He was still hooked up to a respirator because we had decided to donate his organs, so he didn't seem dead. His chest still rose and fell with the rhythm of the respirator and his body was warm. I caressed him, held him, and wept over him. My mother tried to lead me away at one point, but I kept returning to his bedside. Did he know I wasn't beside him when his final moment came? Did he feel alone or abandoned?

These questions tortured me for weeks until, reading one of Elisabeth Kübler-Ross's books, I came across her observation that children often choose to die at a time when their parents are out of the room, for their parents hold them back. Sometime during the night of his father's birthday, Andy slipped away. Perhaps he looked in on us as we were sleeping and whispered a farewell to us. Maybe he also paused along the way to look in on his brother and sisters or a friend or two. Or maybe he awoke in a familiar place before he knew he was even gone. I don't know. Someday I'll ask him.

> *Father, some of us die peacefully in our sleep; others suffer considerably, as your Son did. Yet, regardless of the manner in which we leave this world, we trust that in the moment of our transition, we will be met and overcome by the warmth of your love for us. We will be filled with joy on the day of our homecoming, and we will bless you for finally bringing us home. May our loved ones bask now in the warmth of your Presence, and may they rejoice in anticipation of the day on which we will all be together again.*

Simeon said to Mary, his mother, "And sorrow, like a sharp sword, will break your own heart."
—Luke 2:34-35

When Simeon spoke these words to the mother of Jesus, she was just a teenager, barely out of her own childhood and probably overwhelmed with love for this new child of hers. I doubt that she spent the next thirty-three years worrying much about this obscure prophecy.

On the morning of Andy's death, I was overcome by a sudden urge to get outside of the hospital for a few moments. We had spent the previous week at Andy's bedside and had rarely left the building. I dimly remember hurrying out of the building through a side door and into the blinding heat. My mother, sister, husband, and some friends who had been at the hospital overnight with us followed me. I didn't know where I was going and don't even know why I chose that particular door. But as I walked outside, I saw in front of me a gate leading to a fenced-in yard. I assumed it was the grounds of the convent of the hospital sisters. I don't know why I went through that gate or what I intended to do once inside the shaded grounds.

But as I rounded a corner, I saw directly in front of me a large sculpture of the Crucifixion, with life-sized statues of Jesus on the cross and his mother Mary beneath him. It was as if I had been led to this place. I walked away from my family and sat on the ground at Mary's feet. And for a moment, I became the woman beneath the Cross. I went back in time 2,000 years and felt the unbearable pain of watching a beloved son suffer an unbelievably hideous death. I felt the abandonment, the despair, and the fear of that good woman. I imagined her lifting her tear-stained face to the heavens and shaking her fist at God, crying aloud her anguish. I've seen sculptures of the Pieta and know that no artist could ever adequately capture the agony in the face of the Mother of God. And I knew then that she was with me at that moment. She held me and wept for me and for all mothers who had to bury a child. She knew my pain. She had come to experience the words of Simeon's prophecy, but she had also experienced the Resurrection three days later. She is the hope of all bereaved mothers, and all those who know the pain of losing a loved one. I know that she will have a special welcome for us when we return Home.

Blessed Mother, you know so well the pain of loss. In our times of great distress, gather us into your arms and remind us that in your Son's triumph over the grave, we will all live forever with him.

I know all the right biblical passages, including, "Blessed are those who mourn," and my faith is no house of cards; these passages are true, I know. But the point is this. While the words of the Bible are true, grief renders them unreal. The reality of grief is the absence of God—"My God, my God, why hast thou forsaken me?" The reality of grief is the solitude of pain, the feeling that your heart is in pieces, your mind's blank, that "there is no joy the world can give like that it takes away" (Lord Byron).

—REV. WILLIAM SLOANE COFFIN, FROM "ALEX'S DEATH" IN *THE BOOK OF EULOGIES*, EDITED BY PHYLLIS THEROUX

When death separates us from someone we love there is a time when we think no one has suffered as we have. But grief is universal. The method of handling grief is personal and universal.

—BILLY GRAHAM, *DEATH AND THE LIFE AFTER*

When I think over his short but happy childhood, how much comfort he was to me . . .
when I can bring myself to realize that he has
indeed passed away, my question to myself is,
"Can life be endured?"

—Mary Todd Lincoln

The most vivid feeling I recall from the night Andy died
was the feeling of having been abandoned by God. I
remember sitting on the front porch with our pastor,
Father Kevin Vann, sobbing uncontrollably, crying out,
"Where is God now? I don't feel him anywhere. There's
no sense of comfort!" One person described God during a
period of intense sorrow as an immense glacier. That was a
good description of how I felt that night. I still believed in
God, but I felt as if God had withdrawn from me. He
seemed distant and unfeeling in the face of a pain that
threatened to be the undoing of me, a pain so enormous I
would only be able to grasp it in small segments at a time
for many months.

Father Vann laid his hand on my shoulder that night
and softly said to me, "I think you'll find that comfort
someday." At the time I thought his reply was given
because he could think of nothing else to say. I couldn't
imagine ever being able to be comforted again. It was then
that I understood that lonely, desperate cry from the cross
on Golgotha: "My God, my God, why have you forsaken
me!" Jesus himself felt that sense of utter abandonment,
desolation, and betrayal, the alone-ness of feeling God's
absence. I understood then that the meaning of hell is the
absence of God. Hell became so much more horrible a state
than I had ever imagined as I glimpsed into that realm that
night. I think that God sometimes permits us to experience
what his absence would feel like in order to draw us more
closely to himself, the way a mother might hide herself for
a moment from a child who is wandering away, just to teach
the child how frightening the world could be if he were

22

separated from his loving parent. All the time the parent is watching over the child and knowing that as soon as he cries out for her, she will be right beside him. When I cried out for God, he made himself known to me in a way I had never known him before. Father Vann was right all along. God's absence was only an illusion. God was never more than a heartbeat away from me.

It took me awhile to understand this. I didn't feel God's presence that night or for many nights afterward, but when I had entered as completely as my soul allowed into the darkness of my pain, I realized that I was not alone. I eventually came to know the meaning of a "holy darkness," a time when the pain and the sorrow is all-engulfing and we no longer have even the strength to struggle against the dark. When we are so worn out and exhausted that we allow the darkness to swallow us up—that holy darkness is when we experience God.

Holy God, when you come to us in the darkness of our grief, we are able to see you more vividly than during any of the brightest moments of our lives. It is in darkness and silence that you make yourself known to us most completely. Help me endure my moments of darkness, secure in the knowledge that you are always beside me.

Our God is a God who dwells within, a loving presence near to us who yearns for our happiness, one who walks with us in our struggles. If our God is a God who holds us close "as a mother hen gathers her chicks" close to her

(Mt 23:37), then we will come through our goodbyes with a deeper sense of being tenderly cared for by our God and we will draw comfort and strength from this presence.

—Joyce Rupp, *Praying Our Goodbyes*

Even if a mother should forget her child, I will never forget you. I have written your name on the palms of my hands.

—Isaiah 49:15-16

A few days after Andy died, the parents of one of his friends visited me. This couple had lost a daughter themselves many years ago. They brought me a little statue that had been given to them when their child died. It is a carving of a hand with a child leaning against the palm. At the base of the statue is written the above quote from Isaiah. I've spent a lot of time looking at the little statue and thinking about those words. It's of course unthinkable that a mother could forget her child; indeed my son was about all that I could think of during my waking and sleeping moments. But what God is promising us is that even if such an impossibly outlandish thing could happen—a mother forgetting her child—God could never forget us. I remember when I was a teenager, we girls would often ink onto our palms the names of the boys we thought we were in love with, and we would stare lovingly at the letters that spelled out the beloved's name. The letters themselves were beautiful to us. Think of God's touching love for us. He's written our names on the palm of his hand. He's besotted with love for us. He traces the letters and gently whispers the names of his most precious children.

When at first I would study the little statue, I would repeat the words, "I'll never forget you" to my son. Then I came to realize that I was the child leaning against the carved palm. I was precious to God who knew and felt my pain. It was never out of his mind for a second. He gives us the strength we need to bear up under our burdens, for we are his own.

> *Father, keep me always in the palm of your hand. It is there that I will find peace.*

———————⟨∞⟩———————

There is a sacredness in tears. They are not the mark of weakness, but of power. They speak more eloquently than ten thousand tongues. They are messengers of overwhelming grief, of deep contrition, and of unspeakable love.

—WASHINGTON IRVING

Those who don't know how to weep with their whole heart, don't know how to laugh either.

—GOLDA MEIER

Of all the expressions of human emotion . . . weeping may be the most functional, the most deeply versatile. The tears we weep show us our deepest, neediest, most private selves. Our tears expose us. They lay us bare both to others and to ourselves. What we cry about is what we care about. What we have no tears for hardens our hearts.

—JOAN CHITTISTER, *THERE IS A SEASON*

Tears are the summer showers to the soul.

—ALFRED AUSTIN

I used to wonder if there would ever come a day when I would stop weeping for my dead child. I thought of tears as a reaction to my feelings of deep grief. Gradually I came to realize that the shedding of tears was part of my healing, like a cool salve on a wound. My tears are my gift to myself, a way of physically acknowledging the love I have for my child, a way of saying, "I love you to the innermost depths of my being." Tears have an almost spiritual healing power, an expression of deep love for the ones for whom we weep.

During a conversation the other day with my oldest daughter, Jill, she was recounting a weekend that she had recently spent with some cousins. During this weekend she was introduced to a friend of theirs who had recently lost her mother to cancer. Knowing that Jill had suffered the loss of her brother, this young woman sought Jill out sensing that in her she might find someone who was familiar with the grief she was experiencing. She told Jill that her husband became very upset when she cried and tried immediately to distract her. Jill was able to reassure her that she needed to cry as often and as loudly as she felt. Jill told her to go sit alone in her car if she had to, but never to try to stop the tears from coming.

The tears will dry up in their own good time, but until that time, our tears help to heal us and should be welcome in our lives and not something to dread. There were many times when I felt as if my tears had sprung from a place so deep within my soul that I had not known of its existence. Yet after yielding myself to the tears, the groaning and sometimes screaming sobs, I always felt a gentleness come over me, a soft peacefulness, as if a toxin had been released from deep within me, soothing and purifying me. My ability to weep when I needed to was a healing gift.

Let your tears flow when you feel them welling within you. It is a blessed and sacred release. Tears are cleansing and healing. Like a sudden summer rain shower, when the sun peeks through once again after the cloudburst, so will you feel at peace after a good crying spell. Visualize your tears washing away the dark stain of sorrow on your soul. Cry for all that you have loved and lost, give yourself over to your grieving and let it expend itself. It is the suppression of grief that causes a festering in your soul. Acknowledge your pain, give it to God, and let it go. You will feel wonderfully refreshed and at peace.

> *Lord Jesus, you yourself wept tears of sorrow when you encountered the death of your beloved friend, Lazarus. Be with us in our times of weeping. Remind us that our tears belong only in this life and not in the one you have promised us to come. Let our tears, which we offer to you, heal us, and let us feel the peace of your loving presence. Those who grieve deeply have also loved deeply, and I thank you for giving me the gift of a deep and abiding love.*

The tears streamed down and I let them flow as freely as they would, making of them a pillow for my heart. On them it rested.

—St. Augustine, *Confessions*

In the early days of my grief, I was amazed at the quantity of tears my body produced. There were times when I wondered at how vast this reservoir of tears must be, how I could weep until it seemed I could weep no longer, only to continue crying. I cried in the car, in the grocery store, in church, at restaurants, in bed, in the shower, everywhere

I happened to be. There were many times I begged God to give me the strength to withhold the tears, times that I was embarrassed to be seen crying, but my tears had a will independent of my own.

Now I thank God for those tears. They are cleansing, purifying, and healing. Tears are a release of all the grief and pain within us. They are a healing balm for our spirits. People who don't understand the healing properties of our tears are often uncomfortable with them. They try to distract us from our sorrow and encourage us not to cry. If they only knew how important it is for us to weep and to be healed by our tears. It is those who are unable to cry who are to be pitied. Those who bottle up the poisons of sorrow and grief within them and allow no outlet are the ones whose pain will not heal.

Lord, you wept many times when you walked this earth. You shed tears of sorrow, tears of loneliness, tears of desolation. Your tears gave you the strength to rise above your own pain and accept the will of the Father in all things. Thank you for the healing gift of tears. As they cleanse our spirits, let us also echo your words to the Father: Thy will be done.

No one ever told me that grief felt so like fear.

—C. S. LEWIS, *A GRIEF OBSERVED*

Grief is heavy. It can wear us down. It's okay to be gentle with ourselves when we're going through change and grief. . . . We do not have to expect more from ourselves than we can deliver at this time. We do not even have to expect as much from ourselves as we would normally and reasonably expect.

—MELODY BEATTIE, *THE LANGUAGE OF LETTING GO*

I learned that when people described their feelings as "painful" it was not a metaphor. I felt pain beyond anything I could have possibly imagined: pain so searing it raised goose bumps on my arms, made me nauseous, left me panting and wondering how soon I could die so I wouldn't have to feel it anymore. I learned that I could live, work, and love in spite of excruciating pain. And what's more, a lot of very ordinary looking people are out there, more than I ever suspected, who also live with extraordinary wounds. Time and care do temper the pain. It is not always as sharp, but it is always there.

—ANNE MCCRACKEN AND MARY SEMEL,
A BROKEN HEART STILL BEATS: AFTER YOUR CHILD DIES

At some point . . . your grief may be so all-encompassing that you wonder how the rest of the world can continue to function. You will marvel that buses are running, telephones are ringing, newspapers are being delivered, and people are eating meatball sandwiches. Meanwhile you feel that you've been swallowed up by a whirlpool.

—ELIZABETH MEHREN,
AFTER THE DARKEST HOUR THE SUN WILL SHINE AGAIN

29

With reality comes pain, and the pain, when it comes, is stunning. The pain is actually physical, mostly in your stomach and chest. Your chest feels crushed and you can't seem to catch your breath. I remember feeling pinned like a butterfly and somehow eviscerated. One woman drew an arc that started at her head and ended at her knees and said, "His death was cut out of here."

—ANN FINKBEINER,
AFTER THE DEATH OF A CHILD:
LIVING WITH LOSS THROUGH THE YEARS

When my grief was new it terrified me. The powerfulness of its grip took my breath away and left me gasping for relief. During those first weeks of grief I felt as if my chest had been blown open, leaving a huge gaping wound. I remember experiencing the sensation of not being able to draw a full breath. I didn't realize it at the time, being a new citizen in the world of the grieving, but this is a common experience for the bereaved. One man described it as a feeling of having two concrete blocks tied around his shoulders and being forced to carry that weight. It is a real physical discomfort.

This discomfort is a reminder of how closely united our body and soul are in this life. Deep spiritual pain, sorrow, and mourning have physical manifestations. It's what a broken heart feels like. Only the passage of time has shown me that the intensity of the grief does indeed abate. I was in error to believe I would never laugh or ever embrace life again. Time has lessened the pain. Acceptance has eased the weight on my chest. My love for my son has softened the harsh edges of pain with tender memories of happy moments. I can look at his picture and smile, and the painful clutching that once grasped at my heart has weakened. I will always be the mother of this child. His death did not end that relationship, his absence from this world does not separate our spirits or break the ties of our love. And if there is a wound in my heart that is cold and scarred and will not heal, it is not a wound that disables me. For every time I feel that scarred area of my heart, I remember that only the fire of an intensely burning love could have made such a mark on me, and the fire of that love is more powerful than the scar it left.

> *Jesus, when you rose from the dead, you showed your wounds to your followers to prove to them that you who loved them and had lived among them still lived on. The wounds of our losses live on in us to remind us that the same love that invites the wounding also heals. Our scars remind us that we have loved. Your scars remind us that we are beloved. Draw us near to you, and help us to remember that we will also return home someday to the place where you have promised us that "every tear will be wiped away."*

Only when grief finds its work done can God dispense us from it.

—Henri Amiel, journal, 1882

I had always thought that I was pretty much in control of my life, my feelings, and my emotions. If something was bothering me or causing me to worry, I dealt with it or could put it aside for a while. Grief allows for no such niceties. It is all-consuming. I suppose I had naively once thought that if someone I loved were to die, I would allot a certain amount of time for mourning the loss, and then

I would pick myself up and go on with my life. I'm not sure if I really thought this, because I didn't ever give any thought to the idea of a loved one's death. I was therefore unprepared for the stunning blow that grief actually was. For at least a year after Andy's death, every waking moment of my life was influenced by my grief. Even when outwardly I might have appeared to others to be dealing well with the loss, my inner thoughts were taken up with the death of my child.

There's no shortcut through the minefield of grief work. We must experience every sorrow and every hurt fully, and sometimes we must experience them over and over again. Grief will relax its grip on us only when all of our grief work is completed. This may take a week, or a month, or the rest of our lives. It's only when we begin to accept our state of grief and lean into it, and embrace it as part of our being, that the pain will begin to ease. We can only be patient with ourselves during this difficult part of the journey.

Lord, walk with me on this lonely path of my grief. My loved one is forever in my thoughts and in my prayers. May your promises of everlasting life and your pledge to never abandon me be sources of strength for me each day.

Compassion for myself is the most powerful healer of them all.

—Theodore Isaac Rubin

Good grief means really giving in to the pain. It means that if you want to cry, you cry. If you want to sob, you sob. If you want to close your bedroom door and pound your pillow while you cry and sob, you do that, too. And you do not have to make amends for this kind of behavior.

—ELIZABETH MEHREN,
AFTER THE DARKEST HOUR THE SUN WILL SHINE AGAIN

From the time I was a child I have been cautioned against self-pity. Feeling sorry for oneself was a weakness not to be tolerated in our family. So, several weeks after Andy's death, when I realized that I was mired in self-pity, feeling deeply sorry for myself, I assumed an added burden of guilt. Then one day I realized that self-pity is not necessarily something to despise. A terrible thing had happened to me. I had lost a beloved child. If it had happened to a friend, my heart would break for them. So why should my heart not break for myself?

I then allowed the waves of self-pity to roll over me. I treated myself very tenderly, putting no expectations or demands upon myself that would add to the burden of the day. I gave myself completely over to the task of grieving and laid wide my broken heart for all to see. I permitted myself to cry when I needed to, scream when I felt like it, and to do as much or as little as I felt like doing in one day. I pampered myself in my grief in a way that I had never allowed before, and aided in my own healing.

Lord, be patient with me on those days when I can't seem to function. Lend me your strength and your courage. Shield me with your compassion and walk with me when I stumble.

Life is eternal. . . . Death is but an inevitable transition that each soul makes when it leaves the physical body. It is a freer state which does not limit the soul to time and place

—BETTY BETHARDS

But please: Don't say it's really not so bad. Because it is. Death is awful, demonic. . . . What I need to hear from you is that you recognize how painful it is. . . . To comfort me you have to come close. Come sit beside me on my mourning bench.

—NICHOLAS WOLTERSTORFF, *LAMENT FOR A SON*

It is hard to have patience with people who say "There is no death" or "Death doesn't matter." There is death. And whatever is matters. And whatever happens has consequences, and it and they are irrevocable and irreversible. You might as well say that birth doesn't matter.

—C. S. LEWIS

Even those of us who have great faith in eternal life and are convinced that our departed loved ones live on in God's warmth in heaven, even we are stung by the cruelty of death. We may be reassured by the hope of eternity, but it doesn't completely take away the pain of losing a beloved.

Death is a very difficult fact of our lives. We need to acknowledge our pain and to speak of it. We need to remind others that we have suffered a great loss, and we need to hear from others that our pain is legitimate and real. We don't want to hear that our suffering is God's will or God's test. We don't want our grief to be suppressed when someone asks us to try to rejoice because our loved ones are in a "better place." We need time to mourn our loss and time to question God, time to vent our anger or hopelessness. Death hurts the living and we need to speak of that hurt.

Fortunately for us, God understands all of our feelings and walks with us during this time of our lives. My mourning song today is a song of sorrow, a song of loss, of loneliness and longing for the beloved who has died. The God of love hears my song and carries its melody deep within his own heart. And in response, he sings to me a song of hope. And the soft notes of his refrain soothe my troubled soul.

> *God of love, your song of hope gives me strength to face each new morning. Never let my ears become deaf to your gentle melody.*

Come to me, all of you who are tired from carrying heavy loads, and I will give you rest.

—MATTHEW 11:28

S oon after Andy died, I started seeing a grief therapist. During the first few sessions, I didn't do very much other than sit in her office and cry for the allotted hour. Yet somehow, an hour of unrestrained crying was very cleansing, almost like the sunlight peeking from behind the clouds at the end of a storm. After an hour of crying, I felt a lifting of the burden for a while. I read an article somewhere about the composition of tears. It seems that the chemical composition of tears induced by grief is different from tears brought on by joy, excitement, or allergies.

Our friends and relatives are very tolerant of our tears in the early days of our grief, but as time passes they seem to become more and more uncomfortable with our sorrow. They want us to be well, recovered and whole again, and sensing this, we often try to stifle our grief when we are around others. I especially remember trying not to cry in front of my children because I didn't want to add to the burdens they were already overwhelmed with, but sometimes the tears would come unbidden.

People often seem afraid for us, as if our tears were an indication that we are not recovering or that we are relapsing in our grief journey. If only they understood how healing tears actually are. It is important that we not allow anyone to try to rush us through this time of grieving. There are no shortcuts. We must allow ourselves to give in to our feelings of sorrow. I was commiserating with another bereaved woman one day when she blurted out, "This grief is like a brick wall. No matter how hard I throw myself against it, I can't break it down." I answered her, "Don't throw yourself against that wall. Just sit beside it and lean against it and rest there until you feel better."

> *When all else has failed, we know that we can lay our burdens at your feet, Lord. Our friends and loved ones can comfort us to a certain extent, but it is only at your side that we can truly find peace. Lord, you calm the fiercest storms. Quiet the storms of sorrow within us and give us the rest we will only find in you.*

We must be consumed either by the anger of the storm god or by the love of the living God. There is no way around life and its sufferings. Our only choice is whether we will be consumed by the fire of our own heedless fears and passions or allow God to refine us in his fire and to shape us into a fitting instrument for his revelation, as he did Moses. We need not fear God as we fear all other suffering, which burns and maims and kills. For God's fire, though it will perfect us, will not destroy.

—THOMAS CAHILL, *THE GIFTS OF THE JEWS*

If thou can be still and suffer awhile thou shalt without doubt see the help of God come in thy need.

—THOMAS À KEMPIS, *IMITATION OF CHRIST*, 1441

We can't pray that God will make our lives free of problems; this won't happen, and it is probably just as well. . . . But people who pray for courage, for strength to bear the unbearable, for the grace to remember what they have left instead of what they have lost, very often find their prayers answered. They discover that they have more strength, more courage than they ever knew themselves to have. Where did they get it? I would like to think that their prayers helped them find that strength. Their prayers helped them tap reserves of faith and courage which were not available to them before.

—HAROLD KUSHNER,
WHEN BAD THINGS HAPPEN TO GOOD PEOPLE

It came as a bit of a shock to me to find out that Rabbi Kushner was correct, that we really cannot pray for a life free of problems and sorrows. I read Kushner's book, about his journey of faith after the death of his young son, many years before the death of my own son. I was very moved by his book at the time, but I didn't know then that I would one day walk the same path that Kushner had traveled. There was still a part of me that believed that if I prayed hard enough for something, it would be given to me. Doesn't it even promise in the Bible, "Ask and it shall be given to you"?

Andy was in a coma for a week before his death, a week during which I prayed frantically for his recovery. I was sure that my belief in God was strong enough that my prayers would be answered. I had no doubt that God would heal my son. When Andy died, I was almost overcome with a blinding, searing anger. I was furious with God. I didn't for an instant doubt his existence, but I believed that he had toyed with me for a week, led me along, and then abandoned me. I felt totally forsaken in my grief, apart from the Source of life and love. I didn't understand how my prayers could have been so completely disregarded by God.

We may never understand why some of our most fervent prayers appear to be unanswered, why some of our greatest desires go unmet, or why some of our noblest goals remain unattained. These are times that try our faith to its limits. We are tempted to believe that if God doesn't respond to our needs as we see them, then God either doesn't exist or just doesn't really care about us.

Over the course of the next several months, however, as I searched for meaning in this tragedy, I found that God had not abandoned me. He had held me and felt my tears and suffered with me. He didn't answer my prayers for Andy's return, but he gave me the strength to endure the loss.

I wrote a poem shortly after this realization came over me:

THE JOURNEY

Oh God, my God, did you abandon me?
Did I suffer his death alone?
Did you look away when your own Son died?
Were you far away on your throne?

I searched for you to demand him back,
I pleaded, I begged, for I knew
That if I could mount a proper attack
My prayers would be heard by you.

But he slipped away while the world he knew slept
And you watched his soul set free,
And while I knelt at his bed and wept
You turned your back on me.

You left me alone in the darkest of night,
You left me to cry in vain
And welcomed him into your heavenly light
While I stood alone in my pain.

I damned you, I cursed you for taking my son,
My child, my heart and my soul,
But you came to me when that day was done
And told me I'd needed to know:

That you held me that night
when my world turned black
And your tears burned down on my face.
You promised you'd never have turned your back
Or let me falter in your embrace.

You felt my pain and you wept my tears,
You sheltered me from the storm
Of hopeless despair and blackest fears
You kept me close and warm.

You turned to the East and showed me the dawn
And promised the warmth of a day
When all of our sorrows and pain would be gone
And all of our tears wiped away.

You told me for him that his day had risen
And in your home he'd now dwell.
He'd flown from the bonds of his earthly prison
And you promised to love him well.

You vowed that you'd hold me until my dawn broke
And you never would leave me alone.
Your burden how easy and tender the yoke
Of the journey now leading me home.

Suffering is a test of faith . . . if God's love calls
you in suffering, respond by self-surrender, and
you will learn the mystery of love.

—J. MESSNER, *MAN'S SUFFERING AND GOD'S LOVE*, 1941

The essential mystery of the cross is that it
gives rise to a certain kind of loneliness, an
inability to see clearly how things are unfolding, an inability to see that ultimately all things
will work for our good, and that we are,
indeed, not alone.

—JOSEPH CARDINAL BERNARDIN, *THE GIFT OF PEACE*

Cardinal Bernardin, the beloved shepherd of the
Archdiocese of Chicago, wrote *The Gift of Peace* in the
final weeks before he died of cancer. He would certainly
know the mystery of the cross. Shortly before his cancer
was discovered, a disturbed young man, dying of AIDS,
wrongly accused Cardinal Bernardin of sexual misconduct.
Before his death, the man recanted the accusation, but not

before subjecting the gentle bishop to many hours and weeks of anguish. In his book, the Cardinal wrote a very moving chapter of his meeting with the young man, extending his forgiveness, and staying to offer Mass with the dying man who had become alienated from God and the church. Cardinal Bernardin described the meeting as a "manifestation of God's love, forgiveness and healing that I will never forget."

During that dark period and the months afterward when the Cardinal learned of his own terminal illness, he wrote eloquently of the loneliness of the cross. It was not possible for him to see until later that the sorrow he endured because of the unjust accusations did ultimately end in good being done. It was through the Cardinal's loving forgiveness that the dying man was able to reconcile with God.

When someone we love dies, it is hard to see our way through the pain. It is difficult to believe Cardinal Bernardin's conviction that "ultimately all things work for our good, and we are not alone." If we try to hold on to this thought and keep our faith through our time of sorrow, we will eventually be able to see light at the end of our tunnel of sorrow. We will be strengthened and blessed by our trials, and we will become stronger than we were before.

> *Jesus, you knew the loneliness of the cross. In your triumph over that loneliness, you took upon your shoulders all of our crosses that we might never have to walk alone in our suffering. Be with us now, when it is so difficult to see our way.*

I tell myself that God gave my children many gifts—spirit, beauty, intelligence, the capacity to make friends and to inspire respect. . . . There was only one gift he held back—length of life.

—ROSE KENNEDY

A ny parent who outlives a child would understand the above quote from Rose Kennedy, the mother of John F. Kennedy, a woman who outlived four of her children. Two of her children died in plane crashes and two of them were assassinated. No matter how long our children are on this earth, if we outlive them, then they have not lived long enough in our eyes.

When tragedy invades our lives, we often wonder how a loving God could subject us to the hurts we bear. I was very angry with God in the first few days after Andy died. I had thought that his life could have been spared if God had chosen to do so. The fact that God had not chosen to save my son seemed an abandonment to me. God had ignored my needs, I thought.

I still don't understand why I was called to experience this great sorrow, but I now know that I was not asked to suffer it alone. God was with me with every breath I took, surrounding me with his love, and protecting me from despair. I often wonder if I would have ever come to know and experience God's deep love if I had been spared tragedy in my life.

Father, you are always beside us, even when we doubt your existence. You wait for us to call out to you, and you show yourself to us in our neediness. Never let me forget your presence. Let me always remember your faithfulness and your love.

> In a BBC interview in the 1970s, Jung was asked if he believed in God. He answered just like the experiencer he was: "I don't believe, I know."
>
> —MALLY COX-CHAPMAN, *THE CASE FOR HEAVEN*

Looking back on my life over the past two years, I think that until Andy's death I merely believed in God. I didn't *know*, as Jung stated so confidently. I hoped that God existed. I had had many intimations of God's presence at times during my life, but I'm not so sure that I was entirely without moments of doubting or wondering.

During the week of Andy's hospitalization, while he lay in a coma, I spent every moment in a frantic state of prayer. I made promises, I begged and bargained for Andy's life. I asked an untold number of saints to intercede for me. Hundreds of people in town joined me in prayer for Andy's recovery. A local restaurant placed "Say an Ave for Andy" on its marquee. I really didn't think God would have the heart to disappoint so many of us. And when he died I felt as if I had run headfirst into a brick wall—that brick wall being God. I was coldly furious with God for seeming so distant and uninvolved in the death of my child. It was only with the passage of time that I became aware of God's very real presence during my most sorrowful times. I no longer doubt God's existence or involvement in my life. I know, as Jung avows, that God is in my life.

> *Father, you gather all of your suffering children into your arms. Even when we aren't aware of your presence, you are nearby. Open my eyes and my heart that I might always be aware of the nearness of your love.*

My wife and I have four children—one in heaven and *three* on earth.

—ZIG ZIGLAR, *CONFESSIONS OF A GRIEVING CHRISTIAN*

The question of how many children I have is still a difficult one for me. On the day of Andy's death, I remember crying out as we were leaving the hospital, "How many kids do I have?" I remember a friend reassuring me immediately that I had four children. A few weeks later I sat sobbing in the office of a therapist, and when the doctor asked me how many children I had, I cried out, "I don't know!" Even now, several years later, it is a painful question for me to answer. If I am in a situation where I feel that the question may come up, I often become uncomfortable. I know that I have one child in heaven and three on earth, but I don't always feel like qualifying that to strangers.

Yet how fortunate I am to believe that there is indeed a real place, heaven, where my son lives, is well, and is a part of my life now and forever. How sad it must be for those bereaved parents with no belief in an afterlife to answer the question, "How many children do you have?"

Blessed Mother of Jesus, we commend our loved ones into your arms. May they always know the warmth of a mother's touch and the joy of being loved and cherished. Remind God's children in heaven of the precious love those of us here on earth still have for them, and ask them to pray constantly for us until we too are in your embrace.

No Christian escapes a taste of the wilderness
on the way to the Promised Land.
—Evelyn Underhill, *The Fruits of the Spirit*, 1942

I had known my share of disappointment and sadness
throughout my life. Just before Andy's death, I was at a
point where I had naively assumed that I had paid my debt
as far as suffering went. I looked around at friends who
were suffering through their own problems and I would
think to myself how fortunate I was. My greatest misfor-
tunes seemed to be behind me. I had endured them and
been strengthened by them. I believed that I was about to
enter the most rewarding time of my life. My children were
healthy, happy, and almost grown. Our financial status was
very good. Life had never looked better, and in the recess-
es of my mind I think I actually believed that all of this
good fortune was a just reward for living a good life.

Then Andy died on a hot sunny day, and my world
began to tilt crazily out of control. Everything I ever
thought I knew about life, death, sorrow, joy, breathing,
weeping, laughter, praying, cursing was called into question. In an instant I was thrown from the comfortable oasis
of the world I knew and into the dark wilderness where
nightmares stalked. I realized that, contrary to what I had
once thought, I had never truly entered this wilderness
before. I might have circled its edges a few times, but I had
never entered its depths. I went unwillingly and angrily
into this wilderness, kicking and protesting each step of the
way. I cursed God for taking my child, I cursed my child
for leaving, and I cursed myself for my powerlessness. And
in the darkness of the wilderness, when all the screaming
and crying and anger were spent, when I was drained and
hopeless, I felt the softest flutter of a gentle breeze whispering through me. I felt the divine touch that can be felt
only in the deepest wilderness of our minds. And I finally
realized once and for all that the wilderness is not an evil
place. It is the place where we encounter the divine.

Shepherd, guide me through the wilderness on this journey. Don't let me lose my way or give in to despair. Remind me of your presence, which will give me strength for the day ahead.

Bereavement is the deepest initiation into the mysteries of human life. . . . Bereavement is the sharpest challenge to our trust in God; if faith can overcome this, there is no mountain which it cannot remove.

—W. R. INGE, *SURVIVAL AND IMMORTALITY*, 1919

Losing my son could easily have shattered my faith in God. There was a period of time for a few hours after his death when I was deeply furious with God. I was astounded that the ocean of prayers sent heavenward begging for Andy's survival had gone seemingly unanswered. I felt myself descending rapidly into that "dark night of the soul." In this period I was so overcome with my sorrow that there were days when I could do nothing but sit quietly and stare into space.

It was during this dark time that I began to understand that God does not "will" for us to suffer. He doesn't send us sorrow. He doesn't send us punishment or grief. God doesn't cause hardships, but he does use the occasion of hardship to manifest himself to us. He shows himself to us as a God of unfathomable compassion and love, a God who will never abandon us or let us down. He is not the maker of our suffering; he is the shoulder we lean on in our suffering. If we can understand this and acknowledge God's true role in our life, then we will forever be open to God's wonderful presence.

*God of infinite compassion, may I
always be confident of your presence.
May I never doubt your love for me,
and may I always turn to you in times
of hardship, knowing that you will be
beside me.*

A knowledge that another has felt as we have
felt, and seen things not much otherwise than
we have seen them, will continue to the end to
be one of life's choicest blessings.

—ROBERT LOUIS STEVENSON

We received hundreds of sympathy cards in the weeks
after Andy died, sometimes fifty or more a day. I
found myself tearing into them as if in a frenzy, glancing
quickly at each one and then tossing it aside. Someone
counseled me to save all the cards and read them later
when my mind was a little calmer, which I did, and I found
great comfort from them. But in those early days, I was
desperately searching for cards from other mothers who
had lost a child, who knew what I was going through, and
who could tell me that things would be all right. There
were precious few of those letters. The ones I did come
across I set aside to read and re-read many times.

When we lose a loved one, we feel abandoned, freakish,
and alone. We seek out others who have walked this road
before. Many people who would never before go for any
kind of group therapy find themselves attending
Compassionate Friends meetings or other bereavement
groups. I searched the Internet for hours to find groups that
could relate to this pain. I was fortunate to know a few other
mothers who had experienced the loss of a child. These
mothers sought me out to offer me comfort and hope.

We should not be alone during this time. We need to hear from others who have been there before us, who can listen to our stories and know what our sorrow feels like. We need to talk about our loved one to strangers, to proclaim to others that our beloved lived and was a real person. Other bereaved people know this and listen willingly. They share their stories also. We help each other by sharing our loss and pain. Eventually we find ourselves on the giving end of this compassion, reaching out to the newly devastated, helping them along, encouraging them, and listening to them.

There is an old song we used to sing in church that had this refrain: "Bear one another's burdens, and share each other's joys, and love one another, love one another, and bring each other Home." This is what our lives are all about.

Lord, you are always present to help us bear the unbearable burdens in this life. Teach us in turn to reach out to others who are suffering and, in imitation of you, bear their burdens.

Hell is the only place outside of heaven where we can be safe from the dangers of love.

—C. S. LEWIS

If we had never loved we would not know what it means to grieve. Our grief is an affirmation of love, a celebration of a precious life, an acknowledgment of the beloved's importance to us.

There have been times when I have asked myself if it would have been better for me if Andy had never been born. If I had never had the joy of loving him, then I would not have had to endure the pain of losing him. But

each time I pose this question to myself, the answer immediately springs into my mind that I wouldn't have traded
one instant of the eighteen years I spent with Andy, even
the challenging teenage years when he was often less than
likable. Each moment, every memory, is a precious gift, a
treasure I will carry forever. If I had not loved him, I would
not have grieved so deeply. But if I had not known him, my
life would have been the poorer.

> *Father, those who love deeply also know*
> *what it means to suffer deeply. How*
> *deep your own suffering must be, you*
> *whose love is endless. When we mourn*
> *we experience a part of your divinity,*
> *and we who mourn are blessed because*
> *we will be comforted by you.*

All say, "How hard it is that we have to die"—
a strange complaint to come from the mouths
of people who have had to live.

—MARK TWAIN

Mark Twain was a bereaved parent. Like many who
have endured the loss of a child, the idea of death for
Mr. Twain no longer had the power to frighten him. When
our loved ones have gone before us into an unknown land,
our fear of that land loses its grip on us. It can be nothing
other than a welcome and hoped for end of a journey, for
that is where our loved ones wait for us.

As Twain implies in the above quote, nothing can be
harder than living. We are constantly faced with challenges,
sorrows, hurts, betrayals, and pain. Yet we cling to this life
with all of our instincts. We look for and see the beauty of
our life wherever and whenever we can. We don't dwell on

our sorrows, but instead we look toward each new sunrise and welcome its promise and its warmth. We count our blessings, we treasure our lives, and we embrace this world with all of our being, a world full of hurt and pain.

How then could we fear a world that our very God has promised us would be wonderful beyond the ability of our eyes or ears to imagine?

Lord of heaven and earth, we thank you for the gift of life. Let us treasure each moment we spend on this earth. Teach us to use our time here well, that we might grow closer to you, and may we look forward with hope and joy to the everlasting happiness you promise us after this time of trial is over.

Ever has it been that love knows not its own depth until the hour of separation.

—Kahlil Gibran, *The Prophet*

How many times during our lives have we lamented, "If only I had it to do over again. . . . " When someone we love dies suddenly, there are lots of "if onlys." We regret not having told the departed more frequently how much they were loved. We wish that the final conversation or visit could have been more memorable or meaningful. I don't remember the last words I actually said to Andy. I'm not sure we said goodbye to each other the last time he walked out the door. He came and went all day long ordinarily. I wasn't thinking thoughts of how much I loved him during that final day before the car accident. Andy didn't occupy my thoughts any more frequently than any of my other children, unless he was misbehaving or we were arguing about something, which was fairly frequently given his age.

Yet after he died, I was overwhelmed with the realization of how much I had loved him, how I missed his face and voice, the lunches when it was just the two of us, our little conversations, all the things I had taken so much for granted. Not until after he was gone from me did I realize what a priceless treasure I had had in him.

It was too late then to appreciate the precious gift that Andy had been in my life. But it was not too late to acknowledge and give thanks for the other gifts in my life: my children and husband, my family, my friends and my health. Now, after losing one of my greatest treasures, I will forever take time to give thanks for the gifts I have in my life.

God, Giver of all good things in our lives, I give you thanks for the blessings and all good things you've bestowed upon me. Help me to continually appreciate the gifts you have given me: those who love me and those I love; my eyesight, my hearing, and my health; the beauty in all nature that you display around us each day. You delight in giving us good things. Accept my prayer of thanksgiving.

Friends say we're brave, we're strong. They mean it as a compliment, and I take it as that. But the truth is we have few options. We can stay bitter. We can put guns to our heads. Or we can struggle to find reasons to live. Mine was my surviving child.

—Anne McCracken and Mary Semel,
A Broken Heart Still Beats: After Your Child Dies

I hated hearing people tell me how strong I was a few months after my son died. I didn't want to be strong. I wanted to curl up in a tight little ball and make a clean break with reality. I was surprised at myself for continuing to do the day to day things I had always done, for going on with my life when my life was so full of pain. I almost felt as if being strong, which I now realize was not a matter of choice but of personality, was a betrayal of my son. When people told me I was strong, I heard them saying, "I could not have survived such a catastrophe. The fact that you did must mean that your loss is not as painful as mine would have been."

I can remember walking through the mall one day with my youngest daughter, staring at the people who were passing us, and thinking, "It would be so easy to just throw myself on the floor and start screaming insanely. What is holding me together? I must look like any other shopper out for a stroll and no one could tell that inside I'm screaming." Thoughts such as these gradually led me to realize that I was not the only one walking through life looking normal who was screaming inside. Perhaps I had passed a dozen people or more that day—average, everyday shoppers—who were carrying around a horrible grief or burden.

I finally realized that strength was another gift of bereavement. Those who were without strength didn't grieve more deeply or love their dead any more than I did.

Those who had nervous breakdowns because they were not strong didn't live in happy oblivion. But without a gift of strength they were unable to move ahead as needed each day to work through their grief. The gift of strength allows us to have hope, to be able to function when our hearts are broken, and it allows us to recognize fellow travelers who are also burdened. Our strength enables us to reach out to each other and share each other's heavy loads and to ease the journey for one another. Now, I no longer curse the strength that I have been given.

> *Father, you give strength to the weak and weary. You are that strength, and because of your presence we will never falter.*

The decision to face the darkness, even if it led to overwhelming pain, showed me that the experience of loss itself does not have to be the defining moment of our lives. Instead the defining moment can be our response to the loss. It is not what happens to us that matters as much as what happens in us. Darkness, it is true, had invaded my soul. But then again, so did light. Both contributed to my personal transformation.

—GERALD SITTSER, *A GRACE DISGUISED: HOW THE SOUL GROWS THROUGH LOSS*

One of the first things I remember saying to Karen, the therapist I had begun seeing for counseling after Andy's death, was, "I don't want my life to be defined as being the mother of a dead child. Right now that's all that I'm about, but I want my life back." The horror of realizing that I had a child who had not outlived me took my breath away. I had become one of the "other" people. "Other" people lost their children, not me. "Other" people became highway statistics, not my son. "Other" people tended graves, not our family. I rejected the notion of becoming one of the "other" people.

It was only when I finally accepted the inescapable fact that I was, however unwillingly, one of "them" that my journey toward acceptance could begin. It was also at this time that I found out that there is no such thing as "otherness." We are all alike, all brothers and sisters. We all have our burdens, our tragedies, worries, and fears. There are many people who have suffered the same loss that we ourselves have, who know what our pain feels like and who are able to reach out from beyond their own brokenness to help us along. In time, we too are able to turn and help those who come after us on the same road. Together, stumbling, reaching out for help, pausing to offer comfort, walking together, we can complete our journey. In the process we learn to love and to be loved much more fully. This is one of the gifts of bereavement.

Lord, use my time of mourning to help me grow in love and faith. Strengthen me so that I might follow more faithfully in your footsteps. Teach me to use this time of darkness to search for the light of your everlasting and faithful love.

Grief has a wizard-like ability to alter its potency. This is one of the amazing qualities of what I think of as good grief, or sometimes, good mourning. It is not that grief suddenly becomes a friendly force or presence. That could never happen. But the very nature of your grief does evolve. It seems to settle into a nearly comfortable spot. It becomes something you're aware of, not always afraid of.

—ELIZABETH MEHREN,
AFTER THE DARKEST HOUR THE SUN WILL SHINE AGAIN

There was a time not so long ago when I had only heard the terms "good days" and "bad days" used in the context of describing the condition of an elderly or dying person. I had never dreamed that at a relatively young age and in a state of excellent health my own days would be divided into "good" and "bad" days. A good day, in the first months after Andy's death, was a day that I was able to do something a little productive, able to go to the mall or the library, or for a walk, and not dissolve into tears. It was a day when I could find myself laughing at something before the horrible fact of Andy's death resurfaced in my consciousness. A bad day was a day I spent in bed crying, drowning in blackest despair, thinking this horrible heavy grief would never leave me, that I would never celebrate anything again in my life. At first the bad days greatly outnumbered the good days. Gradually, the good days started to pull even with the bad ones, and eventually the good days overtook the bad. Now, it seems that I might have bad moments, but rarely an entire bad day.

I firmly believe that in the place we call heaven I have a cheering section comprised of all those I have known and loved in my life. These loved ones of mine pray for my happiness and give thanks for the days that I am joyful. They rejoice with me when I am able to laugh, and they gather around me when I am burdened. Some day I will be in that cheering section also. My greatest desire then will be to see laughter on the faces of the loved ones I will have left behind.

> *God of laughter, you delight in the world you have created. You love the sound of our laughter, for our happiness is a song of praise for creation. I offer you the song of my laughter. Accept it as a song of thanksgiving for this wonderful universe you have created for every living creature.*

When you were born, you cried and the world rejoiced. . . . Live your life so that when you die, the world cries and you rejoice.

—CHEROKEE SAYING

A few years ago we were among the sponsors of a national three-on-three basketball tournament that came to town every summer. Several downtown streets would be blocked off and makeshift basketball courts would be set up for the tournaments. One year my kids and some of their friends were watching another friend's team warming up before their game. Suddenly one of the boys noticed that an elderly, shabbily-dressed man who had been sitting on a nearby park bench seemed to have stopped breathing. The authorities were notified and it was determined that the man had quietly died as he sat there on the bench. An ambulance came to carry him away, but it sat on the street corner for a long time while we awaited the arrival of the coroner.

As I stood with the kids, surrounded by hundreds of people rushing to their own basketball courts or standing around waiting for the resumption of play on this particular corner, I thought to myself how tragic it was for a man to go to his death surrounded by hundreds of youthful, exuberant people, and yet be completely alone in his passing. There was no one beside him to hold his hand and wish him Godspeed, no one to mourn his passing, or to say a final prayer for his soul. I could only hope that this lonely human being was surrounded with love in the next instant of his life, and all of his feelings of alone-ness forgotten.

I remembered this incident shortly after Andy's death when I was writing thank-you notes. I thanked Andy's friends for the gifts they were able to give him in death, the tears they shed, the prayers they offered, the love they shared with Andy in his final days. What a gift it is to be remembered with love when we leave this earth.

> *Father, teach me to live each day to the fullest extent. May I brighten the lives of those around me. May I share in their sorrows and in their laughter. May I be a good and true friend to those around me each day of my life. And if I am missed when I depart this earth, let it be because I brought a bit of your light into the world while I was here.*

Swans, who mate for life, are known to exhibit droopy mourning behavior when their spouse dies. Cheetahs, if their cubs have been devoured by lions, will hover over their dead babies and howl for days on end. But what separates animal mourning from human mourning is that animals lack the capacity to question, to be plagued by the question of "why." They don't have a faith to shake.

—ASHLEY DAVIS PREND, *TRANSCENDING LOSS*

Every religion believes in eternity—another life. This life on earth is not the end. People who believe it is the end, fear death. If it was properly explained that death was nothing but going home to God, then there would be no fear of death.

—MOTHER TERESA

Having faith in eternal life, believing that our loved ones are well and happy in their new existence, knowing that they are still present to us in many ways are all comforting ideas for the bereaved. But even these beliefs do not obliterate all the pain involved in losing a loved one to death. There is still the pain of loss, of yearning for the physical presence of the loved one. Therefore even people of great faith, people who firmly believe in eternal life, and who are able to rejoice for the beloved who are receiving the benefits of heavenly joy, even these faith-filled individuals can know deep sorrow on the occasion of a loved one's death. It is not a denial of faith. It's not a matter of doubt or fear of the unknown. It is simply the feeling of sorrow that the separation brings. Even those who have every reason to believe that the spirits of their departed loved ones remain close by still have periods of intense grief and sorrow.

A strong faith helps the bereaved come to terms with the loss and cope with the fact of death, but the grief is still there. Those who love deeply grieve deeply. Those who have faith in the eternal promises of God will transcend their grief eventually and grow spiritually, but they will still need their necessary period of mourning. People of faith don't make light of sorrow. Instead they embrace the sorrow and recognize that it is their ordained time to mourn.

*God of all seasons, when it is my time
to mourn, be with me. Help me to
bear this burden of sorrow. Remind
me that there is a time for everything,
and when this time of sadness has been
fulfilled, I shall laugh and be joy-
filled again. When I walk with you I
will never carry this sorrow alone.*

I did not get over the loss of my loved ones;
rather I absorbed the loss into my life, like soil
receives decaying matter, until it became a part
of who I am. Sorrow took up permanent resi-
dence in my soul and enlarged it. I learned
gradually that the deeper we plunge into suffering, the deeper we can enter into a new, and
different, life—a life no worse than before and
sometimes better.

—GERALD SITTSER, *A GRACE DISGUISED: HOW THE
SOUL GROWS THROUGH LOSS*

One of the Greek words in the New Testament
for healing implies salvation. Spiritual healing
does not restore a person to the place they
were before the illness. It provides a more
comprehensive health care package. The peace
and healing of God that defies human understanding can bring us salvation and keep our
hearts and minds untroubled—even when they
do not satisfy our analytical inclinations!

—DIANE KOMP, *A WINDOW TO HEAVEN: WHEN
CHILDREN SEE LIFE IN DEATH*

The pain involved in grieving was such an unexpected assault on my entire being. I didn't realize that there would actually be physical pain involved. I remember asking people how long it would take me to "get over" this. I was horrified to hear people tell me that I would never "get over" it. I understood this to mean that this searing pain would never end, and I was never more frightened of anything than I was of the thought that I would have to live out the rest of my life in this horrible state.

Now I'm beginning to realize that "getting over" the loss of my son is something that is never going to happen. That idea doesn't frighten me anymore, though, because I have a better understanding of what it means. The physical pain does subside. The paralyzing grief wanes, the all-encompassing sorrow softens. I will "get over" the grief and the pain and the sorrow in the sense that they will no longer dominate my life. What I will never "get over" is the fact that Andy lived, that he was my child and he brought great joy into the lives of those who knew him. I will not "get over" being Andy's mother, even if he only lived on this earth for eighteen years. I will be Andy's mother for the rest of eternity. I will never "get over" the moments I shared with him, the laughter and the tears. They will always be a part of the fabric of my life and I will remember those days with a smile. I am no longer frightened to think that I will never "get over" Andy's death. Getting over it would mean forgetting that he lived, and I intend to celebrate the gift of his life until I see him again.

When someone we love dies, a part of us is pulled through the veil that separates this life from the next one. In spite of my pain, I have never felt as close to heaven as I did in the months after Andy died. When the spirit heals from a great sadness, the healing process leaves it much stronger, and much more at peace. Instead of facing constantly toward the earth, the spirit, in its healing, reaches toward the eternal.

Father, you have taken the fire of my grief and used it to temper my soul, to strengthen and mold me into a new person. I offer this new life to you. May all of my actions today and from now on reflect a kinder and more compassionate person, a person who follows more faithfully in your footsteps.

The fact that humans can be broken and become stronger at the broken places is one of the most profound and touching of all miracles.

—ASHLEY DAVIS PREND, *TRANSCENDING LOSS*

I remember reading a magazine article a few months before Andy's death. In the article, several celebrities were interviewed and asked to name their worst fears. Some of these "worst fears" seemed pretty shallow to me at the time, and I remember thinking that my own worst fear had always been that something bad would happen to my children. I couldn't even think the word "death." It was too fearsome. I believed that I would lose my sanity if any of my children should die. And then, a few months later, I began living my worst nightmare. I didn't know how I would survive the death of my son. I didn't want to survive it. I was utterly broken to the depths of my soul.

As Ashley Prend writes, it truly is a miracle to feel ourselves in the process of growing stronger in the midst of terrible tragedy. It is with such a feeling of awe that we find ourselves rising from the rubble of our devastation, realizing that we have grown and are stronger and better people than we were before. I am still amazed at times at the strength I have, strength that enabled me to get through these past few years in one piece. This miracle is a great gift from our Creator.

Father, you are always beside us. You give us the gifts we need to get through our difficult times, and you fill our hearts with joy even in the midst of our deepest sorrow, because we know that you are near.

Even Jesus, who lived thirty-three years on Earth, spent only three in active ministry. Think how many more people He could have healed—and how many more divine truths He could have imparted—in another decade or two. But He, too, ministered according to God's schedule.

—James Dobson, *When God Doesn't Make Sense*

Why did Jesus spend only three years in active ministry? Why did my elderly grandmother have to live for ninety-two years when the last three of those years were spent in the unhappy loneliness of dementia? Why did my sister's father-in-law have to linger so long before he was finally released from the painful ravages of cancer? Why did our friends' two-year-old daughter die? Why did Andy live for only eighteen years? I don't have the answers to these questions, but when I read this passage from Dr. Dobson's beautiful book, I sat for a moment and reflected on that first question. Why *did* Jesus spend only three years in active ministry?

On the surface, Dobson's questioning has a certain logic. Jesus could have healed so many more people, gathered so many more believers, imparted so many more truths if he had lived longer. The answer finally came to me. Jesus didn't stay any longer because he didn't need to stay any longer. As a result of those three short years, his word has spread to all nations for the last two thousand years. In that short time, he showed the world that death has no power over us. He proved to us that the Father loves us. He managed to get it done in three years.

Someone once said that if you ever wonder if you've accomplished what you were meant to accomplish in this world, ask yourself this question: Am I still alive? If the answer is yes, then you have not yet completed your task. I believe we live as long as we need to live to accomplish whatever task we have been given, whatever lessons we need to learn, and then we are brought home. I don't know for sure what my son's task in this world was, what lessons he needed to learn or impart, but I do trust that he accomplished them and was allowed to return home.

> *Lord, teach me to have faith in your ways, to trust in your love even when I don't understand your reasons at times.*

This is the hour of lead
Remembered if outlived
As freezing persons
Recollect
The snow—
First chill, then stupor, then
The letting go.

—EMILY DICKINSON

I experience an "hour of lead" each time I hear of another mother who has lost a child. Each loss another woman experiences carries me back to the early hours of my own grief. When I behold their pain-filled eyes I see a window into their souls, and when I look through that window, I see myself sitting in that cold, black room, that antechamber of hell, where God cannot be found. And although my own early days of grief are now receding into distant memory, when I see a newly bereaved mother, I know the heaviness of heart she will be feeling, and the weight she'll feel around her chest when each breath is a labor. I know how delicate her feelings will be, when every thought in her mind will be about her dead child and tears are only a heartbeat from overflowing onto her cheeks. I'm familiar with the demons that will haunt her dreams and jolt her from her sleep. And my pain is no longer just a memory. It comes flooding back and joins the flow of her grief as my cries harmonize with hers, and I no longer remember whether it is her child or mine for whom I'm weeping. I become all mothers who have lost a child and they become me. We weep for one another and will do so until we are with our children once again. This newly bereaved mother is immersed only in her own grief now, but she will one day understand that all bereaved mothers are as one.

Dear Mother of Jesus, pray for all newly bereaved parents. You once stood under your Son's cross and knew the unbearable pain of watching your child die. Give comfort to those who have lost a child this day. May they be strengthened by the fact of your own Son's triumph over death, and his promise of everlasting life. Welcome all of our children into their eternal home, and in your embrace may they enjoy the warmth of a mother's love.

Love in our world is suffering love. Some do not suffer much, though, for they do not love much. Suffering is for the loving. If I hadn't loved him, there wouldn't be this agony. This, said Jesus, is the command of the Holy One: "You shall love your neighbor as yourself." In commanding us to love, God invites us to suffer.

—NICHOLAS WOLTERSTORFF, *LAMENT FOR A SON*

The sorrow for the dead is the only sorrow from which we refuse to be divorced . . . the love which survives the tomb is one of the noblest attributes of the soul.

—WASHINGTON IRVING, *THE SKETCH BOOK,* 1819

I have found out that as I have grieved out of the loss I feel and the sorrow in my heart, my grief is also associated with a tremendous and positive feeling of love for the daughter I have entrusted to heaven. The flip side of this sorrow born of love, then, becomes joy at knowing that Suzan is so much better off now than she was with us on earth. This mix of emotions is often strange and extreme, but . . . neither uncommon nor unnatural.

—ZIG ZIGLAR, *CONFESSIONS OF A GRIEVING CHRISTIAN*

A few months after Andy died, Pat and I had dinner with Mary and Lou Henson. Lou had been the basketball coach at the University of Illinois for many years and was at that time enjoying a brief retirement. The Hensons had also suffered the loss of a son in a car accident a few years before Andy died. At dinner that evening they showed us a treasured letter they'd received from Tommy Lasorda, former manager of the Los Angeles Dodgers, who had also lost a son. In the letter Mr. Lasorda related to the Hensons an answer that he gave to a sports interviewer about his son's death. Mr. Lasorda told the interviewer that if God had told him that he would have the option of having a son who would bring him joy for thirty-three years, but would then die and leave unbearable pain in his absence, or he could choose to not have a son and spare himself the pain, he would respond without hesitation, "Bring on those thirty-three years!"

A few years later, I was introduced to Mr. Lasorda through a mutual acquaintance. During one private moment, I took him aside and told him that I had read his letter to the Hensons and how grateful I was that he had shared his feelings with the Hensons, how much it had comforted them, and how they were thus able to comfort me. For a moment the twinkle in his eyes clouded over as we each acknowledged our mutual pain. Then he gave me a brief hug and said in that gruff East Coast voice of his, "I know it's tough. But you hang on to those eighteen years you had him. They were a great gift."

The pain of losing Andy is far greater than anything I have ever experienced in my life. But the joy of having loved Andy outweighs the pain.

Father, knowing great love means making ourselves vulnerable to experiencing great sorrow. As a Being of infinite love, your sorrow must also have infinite depths. As we expect to

*share in your love, we must also expect
to share in your sorrow. Give us the
strength to bear up under this burden
we all carry together.*

Pain is the source of compassion, and compassion shifts our perspective on pain, which frees us from the fear of death.

—MAGGIE ROSS,
IN *CREATION SPIRITUALITY*, SEPT.-OCT. 1992

Not long after Andy's death, another bereaved parent attempted to comfort me saying, "We now belong to a special club, a club we didn't want to join but we're together in it now." I felt revulsion at hearing her words. I hated having to belong to that club, and I wanted no part of that membership. But none of the club members were voluntary conscripts. We had all been drafted against our wills. Yet as time went on, I resigned myself to this membership and found myself reaching out in compassion to other suffering individuals. I had known the pain of loss and the comfort of a caring hand. I needed to return the favor to others in need. I find that this is a common trait among those who have suffered a great loss. It is a gift that we receive and then pass along to the next person. It is what makes us children of God.

*Jesus, you taught us that whatever we
do to the least among us is as if it was
done to you. When we show compassion to others who mourn or are
frightened or lonely, we comfort you.
If we visit a sorrowing friend, we are
spending those hours with you. When
we try to encourage them and give*

*them hope, we encourage you. This is
what you asked of us. This is what you
declared would determine our final
judgment. You asked of us only that
we love each other in order to be welcomed into your kingdom. Let me follow your commandments each day.*

For everything there is a season, and a time for
every matter under heaven: a time to be born,
and a time to die . . . a time to weep, and a time
to laugh. . . .

—ECCLESIASTES 3:1-2, 4 NRSV

I sometimes have a difficult time when I read stories of
everyday miracles, those heartwarming stories about ordinary people who are saved from accidental death by a seemingly divine or angelic intervention, or coma victims who
seem to rally and recover in the wake of prayer vigils. When
I read these stories, instead of being uplifted by them, I am
more inclined to ask, "Where was my miracle? Didn't I pray
daily for the safety of my children? Didn't we pray fervently
and desperately for Andy's recovery when he lay in a coma?
Were the prayers of others more effective than ours? Why
did our child die when other children were saved?"

The above passage in Ecclesiastes not only answers that
question, but it also gives me great relief. Andy did not die
because his guardian angel was taking a coffee break or
because we didn't invoke the right prayers. Andy didn't die
because God chose to punish him or us for some sin, or
because God wanted to test our faith. God is not some sadis-
tic bully who delights in pulling wings off insects. A God of
love does not hurt his children in this manner.

Andy died because it was ordained even before he came to earth that he would be here for only eighteen years. Sometimes I imagine that Andy only agreed to come to this planet if he could do what he needed to do and get back home quickly. Perhaps before I was born, I agreed to endure the loss of a child so that I could further my spiritual growth. These are mysteries whose answers will not be known to us in this lifetime. But if we understand that everything that happens does so according to God's plan, a God who loves us infinitely, then we will be assured in our faith that all will be well in the end.

Holy Father, I place my life in your hands. Let me have faith in your divine plan, let me believe that your plan was designed in and with the love you have for all of your children. Some days it is hard for me to make sense of what is happening in my life. Sometimes it's hard to understand your plan and feel your presence. On those difficult days, draw especially close to me and help me to grow in faith. Let me remember the words of Ecclesiastes, that everything that happens on this world happens in the time you have ordained. Let me accept your will.

Faith is the bird that feels the light when the dawn is still dark.

—RABINDRANATH TAGORE

> All shall be well, all shall be well, and all manner of things shall be well.
>
> —DAME JULIAN OF NORWICH

Dame Julian was a holy mystic who lived hundreds of years ago in a cloistered community. Her words still have enormous spiritual power centuries after her death. I was immediately struck when I read these words for the first time. They speak of the overpowering love of God for God's children. I can see in my mind's eye a feminine God, wrapping her arms around her suffering child and crooning softly, "All will be well, all will be well, and all manner of things will be well." God is a tender Mother who soothes and heals, who kisses the hurts and holds her crying child until the pain subsides. God feels her child's pain and wipes away the tears. She promises a better day for her beloved: "All shall be well."

I picture a Mother sitting on a porch in an old fashioned rocking chair on a warm spring morning, her child enfolded within her all-loving embrace, and they are slowly rocking back and forth. All the while, this Mother is whispering to her grieving child, promising a better day, promising that the pain will ease, and promising to never leave her precious child alone in this grief. And on some inner level, the child is comforted, and knows that someday all shall be well.

God, our loving Mother, hold us and keep us when we bring our sorrows to you, and let us join our voice with yours as you softly sing your mourning song to us: All shall be well, all shall be well, and all manner of things shall be well.

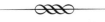

Time of Longing

The woods are lovely, dark and deep.
But I have promises to keep,
And miles to go before I sleep
And miles to go before I sleep.

—Robert Frost,
"Stopping by Woods on a Snowy Evening"

I heard the words of the above poem years ago when I was a child after the death of John F. Kennedy. I remember the feeling of sadness that I felt on hearing the haunting poignancy of those words. It seemed as if our president had so many more miles to travel on this path before he reached the end of his journey, a journey that was cut short before his time. Now, those words seem to suggest to me that death is a beautiful sleep in the "lovely, dark and deep" woods. When we are overwhelmed with sorrow, that sleep can seem a temptation to us, but all of us need to realize that we are not called to rest until our journey is over and our "promises" are kept. It is then, and only then, that we will be invited to that rest.

Father, you alone know how long my journey on this earth will be, and what promises I must keep before being called home to your side. Keep my footsteps steady during this journey and never let me stray from the path you have set me on.

Grief drives men into habits of serious reflection, sharpens the understanding, and softens the heart.

—John Adams

I did not know that Suzy was a part of us. I did not know that she could go away and take our lives with her yet leave our dull bodies behind. . . . I am a pauper. How am I to comprehend this? How am I to have it? Why am I robbed and who has benefited?

—MARK TWAIN, *THE SELECTED LETTERS OF MARK TWAIN,*
EDITED BY CHARLES NEIDER

No one is immune from the tragedies of this life. Suffering and death make no distinction between rich and poor, famous or unknown. When a well-known person such as Mark Twain is seen to have been visited with a grief much like our own, we begin to realize that all children of God are equal. Seeming wealth or fame are not the final rewards for living a good life, and are not guarantees of happiness on this earth. It is in times of our own suffering that we realize that all of our worldly goods are insignificant.

How many of us who are grieving have tried to bargain with God, offering everything we possess if only this death could turn out to have been a bad dream. Yet, people do go on living. Artists and poets have often created great works of art after the death of a beloved. Men have buried their children and gone on to become rulers of nations. Composers have written beautiful music in the throes of grief. Many things of great beauty have been conceived in the womb of great sorrow.

I believe that this is caused in part because during these times of despair and sorrow, we reach out for our Father, and in the reaching we sometimes touch the hem of his gown. And in that touching, our souls are filled with unimaginable beauty and peace which then flows out into our world as poetry or music or great compassion.

*Lord, you know our deepest thoughts
and feelings. When we reach out for
you and are filled with your holy presence, help us to let your love flow from
us and out to all those around us who
are carrying their own burdens.*

God says, "Be silent and listen to me."
—Isaiah 41:1

How can you expect God to speak in that
gentle and inward voice which melts the soul,
when you are making so much noise with
your rapid reflections? Be silent and God will
speak again.
—Francois Fenelon, *Spiritual Letters*, no. XXII

The prayer of a person in mourning is one of the purest
of prayers. It is the laying of a wounded and broken
spirit at the feet of God. It is an emptying of the soul. The
prayer of one who mourns is not a prayer of petition,
thanksgiving, or contrition. It is not really a prayer of
praise. It is just the prayer of a hurting child who climbs
onto the lap and into the arms of the Father. There is no
agenda in this prayer, no needs, no bargains to be made. It
is a prayer of silence, when tears are cried out, when words
have no more effect, and hope seems far off. It is a prayer
that has no words. The time for supplication is over, the
words of anger toward God have cooled, and there is nothing to rejoice over. Words fail. It is at such times that I
found myself just being in a state of surrender to God.
I would simply go somewhere and sit quietly. Sometimes I
went to a park, sometimes to a small chapel. I would empty
my mind and let God's presence fill it. Sometimes, groans

were the only sounds I could make. But even without words, there was communion.

It is in this desert place of our spirit that God comes to his people. He reveals himself in deserts; he nourishes and heals his children in deserts. God makes covenants with his children in deserts and shows his undying love for us when we enter the desert. He soothes and refreshes his children in the dry and barren landscape of the desert. It is only in the desert that humankind is able to see God. And, when we have found our Creator, he leads us into the pastures and lays us down beside cooling streams, and he makes us well.

My prayer today is a prayer of silence, the silence needed in order to hear the whispers of God.

God of the desert, when I empty my soul of all the sorrows and pains in my life, when I am laid bare before you, and the minor problems in life lose their significance; when all the every-day annoyances and worries fade away in the face of my deep weariness with life, then I will find you. I will hear the whisper of your voice and feel the soft caress of your healing touch. I will know your voice and will follow you to the place of my refuge, and you will comfort me and heal me with your love.

Oh Grief, when I had thought me quit of you
You steal so quietly back,
When I believed the sky was blue
And looked, it turned to black.
When pain has softened in my heart
Its edges blurred and dull,
The tears without a warning start
So deeply in my soul.
If I could find that distant shore
I'd leave this lonely place,
If I could see his smile once more
And touch one time his face.

—AUTHOR'S JOURNAL

Today, as I'm writing this, would have been Andy's twentieth birthday. Anniversaries and birthdays are hard for survivors. These dates remind us keenly of those who aren't with us any longer. The memories of once happier celebrations on this date or thoughts of future celebrations that will never be tend to bring our spirits down on these days. We feel our losses more deeply on anniversaries. It is a time to just soften into the pain of the loss. Give yourself time to be with your feelings. Let the memories have free reign in your mind. You have permission to laugh or cry and to spend this day in whatever way is easiest for you. This is also a time to remember that sad days will not dominate our lives forever, but that it is okay to give in to our unhappiness now and then, knowing that the pain will ease up tomorrow.

In the first year of my mourning, a bad day after several good days would frighten me, and I thought that the sorrow would never quit. Now that some time has passed, and bad days are more and more infrequent, I almost welcome the feelings of melancholy that wash over me now and then. They remind me that I grieve because I love, and I am happy to be reminded of this never-ending love I have for my child.

Lord, I remember that you are always beside me. Some days I am busy in things of this world, caught up in life's little worries and pleasures, and I give little thought to your promises. But when I am saddened and burdened with my worries it is good to realize that you are still and always nearby. It is good to be able to lean on your arm when I start to weaken and let you carry my burden when I am tired. Never let me forget your nearness.

My father died in July of 1981. No event in my life before or since so totally destroyed me as that. I remember how very empty the very universe felt and how surprised I was that my father had occupied that much space.

—JULIUS LESTER, "GRIEF," FROM *THE BOOK OF EULOGIES*, EDITED BY PHYLLIS THEROUX

When someone you love dies, you don't lose them all at once. You lose them in pieces, over time.

—FROM THE MOVIE *SIMON BIRCH*

When I heard the above quote from the movie *Simon Birch,* tears sprang to my eyes and I remembered all too well the feeling of losing Andy not all at once, but bit by bit. It's as if the death of a loved one is too horrible to comprehend all at once, and so the realization creeps into our consciousness a little at a time. The empty seat at the table, the telephone that doesn't ring for him, the laundry still in the hamper, the mail addressed to him, the family gatherings where his absence is felt—all of these and so many more daily reminders force us time and again to acknowledge the death. Each reminder is searingly painful, and we gradually, with each reminder, come to realize the enormity of our loss.

I don't believe our minds would be capable of absorbing this loss all at once, and so we part with our loved ones a little bit at a time. After we have gone through this painful period of separating, our relationship with the departed one can become whole again. We come to a point when we realize that we have only lost the physical presence of the beloved. We know beyond a doubt that the bond of love that is shared will never be lost.

Jesus, you told your followers before you returned to heaven that in a little while they would no longer see you. Yet you promised that you would never leave them alone, that your spirit would always be near them and that you would prepare a place for them in your heavenly home. Our departed loved ones have realized this promise and now rejoice for all eternity with you. Keep your promise alive in our hearts until we also are together with you in heaven.

We are healed of a suffering only by experiencing it to the full.

—MARCEL PROUST

Let grief do its work. Tramp every inch of the sorrowful way. Drink every drop of the bitter cup.

—BILLY GRAHAM, *DEATH AND THE LIFE AFTER*

How do we grieve? Awkwardly. Imperfectly. Usually with a great deal of resistance. Often with anger and attempts to negotiate. Ultimately, by surrendering to the pain.

—MELODY BEATTIE, *THE LANGUAGE OF LETTING GO*

When I was three years old, my parents lost a son, my two-year-old brother, Kevin, in a freak accident. I had only a glimmer of an idea of what my parents must have felt until I experienced the same loss forty-some years later. Andy's death was a double loss for all of his grandparents because not only did they lose a grandson, they also had to watch their son and daughter, his parents, struggling with this horrible grief.

My mother and I spoke of our two experiences one day. When my brother died, there was little if anything in the way of grief counseling or support. Bereaved parents were supposed to keep a stiff upper lip and carry on with as little display of emotion as possible. This is what my mother attempted to do for several years, even giving birth to other children in the meantime. Yet it was not until Andy died that my mother admitted to me that she had never grieved properly for Kevin. She had had several breakdowns in the years after his death, at one time leaving our home and wandering across the country for over a year. It was almost half a century later that she was able to admit that Kevin's death had caused her to leave as she had. She had not been able to work through her sorrow in a healthy way and had suffered the consequences for a long time. I don't think her healing started until she became a hospice volunteer some thirty years after Kevin died and took courses in grief management.

Elisabeth Kübler-Ross calls it "grief work," the period of time we must devote to "working" through our pain. We must give ourselves fully to this exercise of grief work. We need to allow and accept all of the associated feelings that we encounter. We need to indulge ourselves, to cry and scream and wallow in this grief, and wade through it, all the while with our eyes fixed on the horizon of our healing. We can only approach that horizon by reaching for it.

Lord, send your angels to guide me through this darkness of grief. I accept this time of grieving for I know it is also a time of growing. And as I grow, let me draw ever closer to you.

It's the *neverness* that is so painful. *Never again* to be here with us—never to sit with us at table, never to travel with us, never to laugh with us, never to cry with us, never to embrace us as he leaves for school, never to see his brothers and sister marry. All the rest of our lives we must live without him. Only our death can stop the pain of his death.

—Nicholas Wolterstorff, *Lament for a Son*

There is a mountain in the distant West
That, sun-defying, in its deep ravines
Displays a cross of snow upon its side.
Such is the cross I wear upon my breast
These eighteen years, through all the changing
    scenes
And seasons, changeless since the day she died.
—HENRY WADSWORTH LONGFELLOW,
FROM "THE CROSS OF SNOW"

After the initial shock of the death of a loved one there comes a period of grief where we deeply miss that person. This is one of the most difficult times of our grief journey.

I remember sitting in my counselor's office a few months after Andy's death. We had previously discussed the shock, the grief, the sorrow, and the unnaturalness of losing a child. On this day, as I sat there, tears softly trailing from my eyes, I said quietly to her, "I miss him. I just miss him." We gradually become aware of the painful truth that this loss is forever.

We can compare death to someone moving to another state, or a child going off to school, but in those instances there is always the hope and expectation of a reunion someday on this earth. With death comes the acknowledgment that there will not be a reunion in our lifetime, and we deeply mourn that empty space within us.

With time, however, and by the grace of our faith in God, we incorporate that feeling of longing for the physical presence of our beloved into a belief in the continuing existence and presence of those who have left us. We know on some level that our loved ones have left us only in the physical form. The essence of our loved ones—their spirits—are forever beside us, and in some ways nearer than ever before. When we reach this point in our season of grief, we finally understand that death does not separate us from those we love.

Lord, before you left this physical earth behind, you promised your disciples that you would never abandon them and that one day they would join you in your heavenly home. You are always near us. Help me to remember that promise today.

Sorrow is no longer the island but the sea.
—NICHOLAS WOLTERSTORFF, *LAMENT FOR A SON*

Sorrow comes in great waves . . . but it rolls over us, and though it may almost smother us it leaves us on the spot and we know that if it is strong we are stronger inasmuch as it passes and we remain.
—HENRY JAMES, "GRIEF DEFINED," FROM *THE BOOK OF EULOGIES*, EDITED BY PHYLLIS THEROUX

Working through the grief of losing a loved one is an enormous undertaking. It uses up much of our energy and most of our waking moments. I have sometimes compared it to attempting to swim across a vast ocean. When we first step into the ocean we begin our grief-journey. We have no other recourse but to swim to the far side. Some days the waters will be peaceful and we can float along and let the tides carry us. Some days we might find ourselves washed up onto a small island where we can rest from the throes of our grief for a while. But eventually we must again enter that vast expanse. Some days will be stormy and we may feel helpless as the waves toss us about and threaten to overwhelm us. During these difficult days we should remember that a Loving Presence always swims along side us, a Swimmer of great strength who will never fail to hold our heads above water when the waves threaten to engulf us, and who will encourage us as we continue our swim toward the distant shore.

There are no shortcuts on this journey. In order to get to the other side we must fully immerse ourselves in the waters of our grief, and we must work with all of our strength and determination to get to the other side. There are days when we ride along the tops of the waves and may be able to see that distant shore, and then there are days when we again feel lost and adrift. But we should never give up hope of eventually finding that shore. Our Companion will show us the way.

> *Lord, stay in my sights always. Without your presence nearby, I know that I shall founder and be lost. Let me be aware of you each moment of my day, and may your nearness calm my fears.*

> When we experience our good-byes, we come face to face with questions about suffering. We also come face to face with a God who suffers pain and hurts with us, a God who wants us to be free of our suffering.
>
> —JOYCE RUPP, *PRAYING OUR GOODBYES*

Not long after Andy died I had a very moving experience. Sean and Jill, my two oldest children, had left for their school, and Julie, who at the age of fifteen was still dealing with her grief, was also trying to cope with the loneliness of suddenly having no siblings in the house with her. I was having a hard time surviving, and I'm sure I was no help to anyone.

One Sunday morning after having spent most of the night tossing, turning, and crying, I went out onto the front porch and sat by myself for a few minutes before we were to leave for church. I was going through a time of being very angry with God, and as I sat on the porch I could feel my anger building. I whispered to my God, "You've been worthless to me. I thought you were supposed to be a God of the suffering. You've completely abandoned me. You haven't suffered with me at all!"

As I was thinking these words I noticed a storm blowing in from the east, which is unusual in our part of the country. Soon the sky was dark and angry and the wind began to blow. "Is this your sign of grief?" I mocked. "You can't even come close to what I'm feeling." Then the rains began and as I continued to berate God, it began raining harder and harder. Suddenly it started to hail, great huge drops of hail that covered the ground. The storm lasted a few more minutes and then died away. But during that time, I felt an awesome sense of the presence of God, and I could feel his suffering. He was suffering with me, and weeping for my sorrow. It was a very moving experience, one I shall never forget.

I realized at that moment that God truly does enter into our suffering with us. I realized then that God did not cause Andy's death. Andy didn't die because someone was being punished or tested. He died because he was a human being with free will and was following the road we all will take. And God suffered deeply to see me suffering so terribly. I knew in that instant that I was loved and that I would never be alone.

A few days later I was reading a book and came across a quote from the Book of Job. In this passage God, speaking to Job, says, "Have you ever visited the storerooms, where I keep the snow and the hail? I keep them ready for times of trouble . . . "(Job 38:22-23). Those words jumped right off the page at me. I had never seen that passage before, but it was further verification that the experience that I had was a communion with God who loves us deeply and passionately.

Father, may we always remember that you love each of us endlessly and totally. Give us the grace to always turn to you in times of pain and sorrow so that we might be comforted by your love.

I have found comfort knowing that the sovereign God, who is in control of everything, is the same God who has experienced the pain I live with every day. No matter how deep the pit into which I descend, I keep finding God there. He is not aloof from my suffering but draws near to me when I suffer. He is vulnerable to pain, quick to shed tears, and acquainted with grief. God is a suffering Sovereign who feels the sorrow of the world.

—GERALD SITTSER, *A GRACE DISGUISED: HOW THE SOUL GROWS THROUGH LOSS*

When sufferings come upon him man must utter thanks to God, for suffering draws man near unto the Holy One, blessed be He.

—RABBI ELEAZAR BEN JACOB, FOURTH CENTURY

I'm not sure that very many of us would care to give thanks to God for sending us suffering. It is, granted, an opportunity to draw closer to God, but how many of us have ever asked to suffer in order to be able to do so? However, it is a lesson that those who are in pain have learned well. There are many men and women who look upon times of sorrow and trial as the greatest gifts they have been given. These are people who have been in prison, people who have received a diagnosis of a life-threatening illness, or who have suffered the death of a loved one. These are men and women who have found that in that time of greatest suffering, when life appears most bleak and hopeless, some powerful force begins to assert itself in their consciousness. It is the realization that, at their lowest and loneliest moments, they are not alone.

When the awesome and loving presence of God makes itself known, it is impossible to feel despair. It is often during such times of suffering that we become spiritually awakened. The powerful presence of God fills us with such peace and hope that we yearn to grow closer to this source of love and consolation. Material possessions and everyday worries that once consumed us begin to have little importance to us. We begin to feel that it is more important to share our sorrows and our joys with those around us, to lift each other up and bring each other home to that place of perfect peace. When we reach this state, then we will be able, as Rabbi Ben Jacob claims, to utter thanks to God for our suffering.

> *Father, in times of our greatest need, you make yourself known to us and show us the depth of your divine and eternal love. Be with us today as we face whatever trials may come our way, and surround us with your peace.*

Time spent in the fog of pain could be God's greatest gift. It could be the hour that we finally see our Maker. If it is true that in suffering God is most like man, maybe in our suffering we can see God like never before.

—MAX LUCADO, *THE GIFT FOR ALL PEOPLE: THOUGHTS ON GOD'S GREAT GRACE*

Last year I attended a bereavement group at our church. During the introductions, an older, obviously lonely gentleman was sharing his distress at the recent death of his wife of nearly fifty years. In attempting to console this very distraught man, Sr. Joann, the moderator, began to recall her memory of the sorrow she experienced at the time of her mother's death. The gentleman brusquely interrupted her, saying, "Sister, that was just your mother. That's nothing like losing a spouse!" In the meantime I caught myself thinking, "But you only lost a wife . . . nothing like losing a child!" I realized that we were trying to weigh our own grief against that of the others in the group, each of us convinced that our personal loss was the most profound.

One afternoon I met my oldest son, Sean, for lunch on his college campus. It had only been a few weeks since Andy's death, and Sean was having a difficult time adjusting. Suddenly he looked up and asked, "How bad is this, Mom?" I answered, "Sean, it's the worst thing that can happen to a mother." Sean replied, "It's harder for me than for you, Mom. I feel like I've lost the right side of my body." I was on the verge of explaining to my grieving son how his sorrow could not match mine, when suddenly he interrupted and said, "Isn't this stupid? We both miss him. How can we even try to compare who's hurting the most?" Then I realized that the pain of loss is not something that can or should be measured by the relationship of the deceased to the survivor.

I had lunch with a very successful businesswoman last fall who spoke to me for a good portion of the meal about the grief she experienced when her dog died. She was quick to admit (maybe not quick enough) that the pain of losing a child had to have been much greater, but nevertheless her sorrow was genuine, her pain was felt in a real way.

It wasn't until Andy died that I began to understand that God feels our pain as deeply, if not more so, as we ourselves do. With God, we don't need to make any comparisons about how great this grief might be compared to another type of loss. The point is, if we are suffering at all, God is right beside us, sharing the moment with us. Friends and acquaintances who were afraid of our grief and uncomfortable around us were not much help to us in the early days of our mourning. The friends who held us and cried as many tears as we did were the ones who strengthened us. A God who cannot enter totally into our suffering with us cannot help us. When I began to realize that my pain devastated God, then I began to see him in a more profound way than I ever had before. God enters our suffering and our rejoicing in a very personal and intimate way. This is a God that I was meeting for the first time.

Father, you constantly remind us that you are near, that you will never abandon us, and that your love for us is all-encompassing. Sometimes it takes a great loss for us to realize this. May our prayer today be one of praise to you for fulfilling all of your promises to us. We praise you for showing yourself to us in our time of greatest need, and we thank you for holding us close during the storms in our life. God of suffering, unite my sorrows

with yours today that I may be puri-
fied by your love.

No dogma of religion is surer than this: if one
would be close to God he must suffer.

—WALTER ELLIOT, *THE SPIRITUAL LIFE*, 1914

The above quote might also be reworded: "If one
would suffer, he must be close to God." Suffering is
meaningless if we are unable to look beyond the pain of
our sorrow and reach for the hand of God to lead us
through it. I have never been as close to God as I am during times of sorrow. The God that we reach out for, the
God who comes when we cry out in the darkness, is the
God who comforts us in our pain and surrounds us with
his love. This is the God who makes his presence felt in the
most profound and intimate ways, a God who enters into
the darkness and walks alongside us. He is not the awesome Ruler of the universe, the King of heaven and earth,
the fearsome Deity of scripture and tradition. This God is
a soft Presence who sits quietly in the darkness with us. His
tears blend with ours. He yearns for us to know him so that
he might console us and draw us to him. In our nights of
sorrow, we are drawn close to the God who loves us.

Walk beside me, Lord. When I awak-
en in the night and feel the pain of my
loss, when I am fearful in the dark,
make your presence known to me.
Comfort me with the knowledge of
your love.

Hope is like the sun, which, as we journey toward it, casts the shadow of our burden behind us.

—SAMUEL SMILES

Now I am beginning to live a little, and feel less like a sick oyster at high tide.

—LOUISA MAY ALCOTT, IN EDNAH D. CHENEY, *LOUISA MAY ALCOTT: HER LIFE, LETTERS, AND JOURNALS*

Each day in our journey of mourning takes us a little closer to the warmth of healing. Some days will find us traveling up hills or down in valleys where the light of the sun is not as warm as other days. Other times we will find ourselves traveling in darkness, times when we doubt we'll ever feel the warmth of the sun again. Mourning is like that. Then, on other days we will feel the full warmth of the sun, and we will for a while bask in its warmth. After awhile, we will learn to dread the night times a little less, knowing that they will pass, and the sun will shine again for us.

A few months after Andy died, I wrote in my journal, "It seems like the bad days are so much 'badder' than the good days are 'good.'" In the early days of bereavement, the bad days are indeed longer and harder. The good days, days we allow ourselves to relax and enjoy life around us, are infrequent. Karen, the grief counselor I started seeing right after the funeral, warned me right away that recovery is not measured as a steady progression. There would be days when I would feel pretty good followed by days that I felt awful. In the beginning there would be more bad days than good. Gradually there would be more and more good days and fewer difficult ones. But I had to accept that there would be times when one minute everything would seem okay and the next minute some thought or memory would plunge me into a black hole. There are lots of dips and turns and curves in the road of recovery from grief.

The important thing is to stay on the road through all the ups and downs of the journey, believing that, as time passes, the days become warmer and the sun brighter and the road easier.

The important thing to remember is that you are never alone on this road. When the traveling becomes too much of a burden, it's okay to stand still for a while, to rest until you are ready to pick up and move on. And whether you are moving or standing still, Someone is with you each moment, Someone who is showing you the way, holding your hand, and resting beside you when you are weary. He wants only your happiness and peace, and he will never for an instant leave you alone on this journey.

> *Walk with me, my Lord and Friend,*
> *Rest me in the peaceful field*
> *By quiet waters at daylight's end,*
> *All my cares to you I yield.*
> *If I stumble in the dark of night*
> *I know that I shall have no fear.*
> *Your rod and staff shall be my light,*
> *You give me strength for you are near.*
> *You prepare a feast for my broken soul,*
> *Our enemies you keep at bay.*
> *You fill my cup till it overflows,*
> *An honored guest at the end of day.*
> *Your goodness and love shall follow me*
> *As faithfully you lead me home*
> *Where I'll live in your house eternally*
> *When all my wandering here is done.*

—AUTHOR'S JOURNAL

There are more things in heaven and earth,
   Horatio,
Than are dreamt of in your philosophy.
                    —William Shakespeare, *Hamlet*

Adversity in the things of this world opens the
doors for spiritual salvation.
      —A. J. Toynbee, in *The New York Times Magazine*,
                                          12/26/54

Even in our sleep, pain which cannot forget,
falls drop by drop upon the heart, until, in our
own despair, against our will, comes wisdom,
through the awful grace of God.
                                        —Aeschylus

One of the great gifts of the Holy Spirit, as I memo-
rized so many years ago in my Baltimore Catechism,
is wisdom. I had always assumed that this gift was something that we would more or less acquire through our own
efforts as we traveled through life studying and learning as
much or as little as we chose.

When my child died, however, and I was forced into
the desert of my grief, I began to realize that from this horrible experience, I had grown in wisdom. I reached out in
the blindness of my pain for something to give me some
relief. And in the reaching out I managed to touch that
mysterious inner world we call the spiritual. While groping
in the darkness of my mourning, my hands brushed against
the Divine and I was rescued. Instead of all of my questions being answered, though, I formed many more questions. I knew then how mired in ignorance I had been all
my life. I finally understood that there is infinitely more to
this universe than we can even begin to conceive. It is a
part of our journey on this earth to come to know more
about our spiritual self. Sometimes, as was the case with

me, we must meet with great tragedy before we feel the need to begin this quest. But once the search begins, our lives will never be the same.

I'd learned much more about living and dying, about loving and losing and finding again. I'd learned that God is unfathomable, but within those unfathomable depths was a burning, consuming love for me. Within this God who defied all understanding, dwelt great suffering, a Guardian of all of our pain and our tears and our hopes and needs. I'd learned in my grief that God is so vast that we will not be able to understand him in this lifetime, but we will be able to feel his love for us, and we will be able to find peace within him. This wisdom was given to me, not to reward me for having suffered the loss of my son or to make up for his death, but to help me deal with it, to help me to try and make sense of my pain. Finally I was able to understand how wisdom could be a gift.

Holy Spirit, one of your divine gifts is the gift of wisdom. I see my own ignorance and long to accept your holy gift and to grow in knowledge. Be with me and guide me along this path today. Everything I learn will bring me closer to your Divine Mystery. Be my Teacher now and forever.

Call on God, but row away from the rocks.

—Indian Proverb

God is always near us, ready to catch us if we start to stumble; but in order to experience growth in this grief journey we must make a conscious effort to heal and move forward. It is hard sometimes to tell yourself to move on.

There were too many days when I would have loved to just stand on a street corner and go stark raving mad, with God and man as my witnesses, to scream out for all the unsuspecting world to hear about this awful hell of losing a child. It was hard to be in a crowd of people smiling, nodding, and interacting in ordinary ways with others when I was inwardly wailing in grief.

The belief that the passage of time will ease the pain is an oversimplification. We must also work at this healing. We must sometimes force ourselves to go to the grocery store or to church or to a party. Life will only become easier if we make the effort to bring order back into our lives. There is no set time for recovery from grief. There is no straight progression, but instead a few steps forward and a few more back until we become more familiar with this path. The important thing is that we take the first step on our own, with the determination to continue on this journey of life in the manner which God has planned for us.

Be my companion on this journey, Lord. Walk with me through hard times and happy times. When I am tempted to look back or am tiring of the struggle, guide me with your gentle hand. When I'm reminded of your unfailing love for me, I am strengthened and filled with hope.

God uses grief to heal us, strengthen us in our faith, and cause us to grow in our relationship with him. While I do not believe that God caus- es the circumstances that result in our grief, I do believe that God uses grief as a process to show his compassion toward us, to teach us, and to bring us into greater wholeness.

—Zig Ziglar, *Confessions of a Grieving Christian*

God can set us right only by breaking us down. As long as we remain in a self-assured, right- eous, left-brain position, there is no way we can be bridge builders or reconcilers.

—Richard Rohr, *Job and the Mystery of Suffering: Spiritual Reflections*

I knew how Humpty Dumpty must have felt: I was shat- tered and none of the king's horses and none of the king's men would ever be able to put me back together again. It was not until the tough outer shell around me cracked open that I was able to realize how that thick shell had also prevented many graces and blessings from pene- trating to the core of my being. With that hard outer shell, I was able to keep God at arm's length. I allowed God a few prayers a week, mostly prayers of petition. I tossed lit- tle crumbs of myself to charities, and attended the obliga- tory church services on Sundays. But, beyond that, I was happy to have God keep a polite distance, in kind of a "don't call me, I'll call you" relationship. I think I was afraid of the demands he might make upon my soul if I were to allow him closer access to my life. My life, as I saw it before Andy died, was just fine thank you, Lord.

And then I fell off the wall. It is true that the king's horses and his men were pretty useless as far as reconstruc- tion was concerned. But then the King himself came along. He gently and lovingly picked up the broken pieces, and with his artist's hands he crafted a new me. Gone was the old hard shell. In its place was a soft covering that fits so comfortably over all the bumps and bruises, all the aches and pains, a covering that allows healing in. And there in all my vulnerability, God found a soft spot, a breach in my defenses, and he found a way to come in. I certainly didn't enjoy falling off that wall. The pain was tremendous. I was comfortable in my old shell, and I wept to see it broken. But the King put me back together much more beautifully than before.

Father, you break our hearts of stone. Re-create us with hearts meant to love you.

Sometimes God lets you and me struggle until we recognize our dependence on Him. In so doing, He gives our faith an opportunity to grow and mature.

—JAMES DOBSON

The Lord would have us know that sorrow is not a part of life; that it is but a wind blowing throughout it, to winnow and cleanse.

—GEORGE MACDONALD

I believe that it is hard to develop a deep relationship with our Creator when we are fully immersed in this life. When our lives are going smoothly, when we feel that our life is one big vacation, or heaven on earth, we may consider ourselves to be prayerful and devout people. But it has been my experience during those times that my prayers tended to be prayers of thanksgiving, prayers of praise, prayers—in other words—asking God not to disturb the status quo. We're saying, "God, everything's great here just like it is. You must be rewarding me for something good I've done. I'll try to keep on being good and you just keep the good times coming. Thanks for everything." I never really attempted to hear God's whispering. I just wanted to keep him off my back.

But it is during times of trial that we truly begin to experience the Divine within and around us. When the shallow delights of this world no longer hold any happiness for us and our spirits turn inward in despair or loneliness or sorrow, then our spiritual ears and hearts are finally opened to encounter the love of the Creator. When worldly riches and treasures cease to be sources of comfort and we reach out in our blindness and our pain, it is our Father's arms into which we find ourselves falling. It is then that we really begin to have a relationship with our God, our God who comes to us in the silence of heartbreak and despair, who holds us and heals us.

> *Creator of all things, in the silence of my sorrow, my eyes and ears are opened to witness your unfathomable love, to listen to your voice and rest in your being. Create a silent place within me where I will always be aware of your presence, and where I can go to hear your voice.*

It has taken me a long time to recognize that darkness is an essential element for personal growth. No matter how many "right things" I do, darkness will still come unannounced and uninvited because it is an essential part of life. Without darkness I cannot become the person I am meant to be.

—Joyce Rupp, *Little Pieces of Light*

Like everyone else, I've experienced periods of darkness in my life. Some times were harder than others, but until my son died I had never really experienced the darkness of losing a loved one to death. I had buried my grandparents who had lived to ripe old ages and had died peacefully. Although I missed them and loved them, their deaths had seemed to me to be in the normal course of life events. Nothing in my life had prepared me for the darkness of losing a child.

And it was not until I entered into this darkness, that I realized that this is where spiritual growth occurs. We are creatures of light. We yearn for light in our lives, we need it to live. Yet it is in darkness—when all of our distractions are silenced, when our souls are laid open, and sorrow consumes us—that we reach out in our neediness for solace. It is in darkness and silence that we first hear the soft whisper of the Divine, and it is only when we have experienced darkness that we can understand the wonder of light. It is only in experiencing darkness that we learn to grow toward life-giving light.

> *Father, you come to us in darkness and in silence. Still my busy spirit when life seems to be rushing by me at too fast a pace. Calm my soul and allow me to experience the peace of your presence.*

Your pain is the breaking of the shell that encloses your understanding. Even as the stone of the fruit must break, that its heart may stand in the sun, so must you know pain.

—KAHLIL GIBRAN

When I am feeling the pain of losing my son, I need to remind myself that the sorrow and suffering that I experience are God's gifts. They may be unwelcome and unwanted, but they are nevertheless gifts. Pain is a gift that causes us to grow toward God. In our pain we are much like a seed that is forced to burrow through the darkness of the earth in its quest for the life-giving warmth of the sunlight. If the seed is to grow and flourish, it must force its way through the cold darkness of the earth until it bursts into the light. If we were never planted in the dark earth of pain, we would never know the longing for Light. We would not yearn for God if we had never known separation from him.

Our prayer today is one of longing for the comfort that only God can bring us. In the darkness of our sorrow, we reach for God and we are unfailingly brought into the warmth of his embrace.

Father, I turn to you in the midst of my sorrow. It is only through you that I will find solace. Carry this burden for me awhile and let me rest in the shadow of your presence.

Be merciful to me, O God. . . . In the shadow of your wings I find protection until the raging storms are over.

—Psalm 57:1

Even when life does not make sense, God has not lost control of our lives. He wants us to trust Him. His presence is very near.

—James Dobson, *When God Doesn't Make Sense*

One of my most tender memories of Andy is when he was about eighteen months old. He would wake up crying during the night, and I would hear this plaintive little voice calling out, "Mommy?" When I'd answer him, he'd cry out, "I wanna rock-a-bunting." In the middle of the night I would get up and go into his room where I would rock him back to sleep singing "Bye, Baby Bunting" until he drifted off.

God is like a parent in the middle of the night. When we are in the darkness and we are confused and frightened, God comes to our sides at once. He takes us in his arms and gently rocks our troubled spirits. Andy didn't need to be held for long; sometimes it was just for a few minutes, but in those quiet moments when he rested peacefully against my breast, I can still remember the feelings of love for this child that washed over me and bathed him in my love. God feels that way about me. He is always nearby, always listening for my call, and eager to put my tired soul to rest.

Father, when we call out to you in the darkness you hurry to our side. You fill us with comfort and peace. You give us rest and strengthen us for the coming day. When I am frightened, you are beside me to give me courage, and when I am despairing, you give me hope. Your love is perfect and without flaw. You never abandon your children. You are beside us always, even when the darkness is so deep that we cannot see you, and our cries are so loud that we cannot hear you. Teach our frightened souls to listen for the sound of your soothing whispers of love.

I will comfort them and turn their mourning
into joy, their sorrow into gladness.

—JEREMIAH 31:13

We don't go to God as a way to ignore our
pain [but] to give Him our pain, that we might
soften around it as we relax into our trust in
Him. We then become bigger than the pain,
and thus able to absorb it.

—MARIANNE WILLIAMSON, *ILLUMINATA*

I t was so easy to blame God for the death of my son during the first few hours after we learned that he had died.
I was very angry with God for having turned a deaf ear, as
I saw it, on my pleas for Andy's life. I blamed God, not so
much for causing Andy's death, but for standing by and
doing nothing to prevent it.

When I look back, I realize that I was fortunate to be
able to express all of this anger toward God. If I hadn't had
faith in his existence, I couldn't have been angry with him.
Some people in their grief lose their belief and faith in
God. I was lucky because even though I was extraordinar-
ily furious with him, I remained open to and willing for the
possibility that if anyone were going to salvage this situation, it would take a Being no less than God. In my anger
I waited for him to make himself known to me, to reach
down and touch my broken spirit. And when eventually I
felt his healing touch upon my heart, I knew that I would
never carry this burden alone. He had not abandoned me
as I had thought. He had surrounded me with his love and
protection.

*Father, I bring you the burdens of the
day and lay them at your feet. Let me
rest in the comfort of your loving presence. Give me the strength to walk this*

path of mourning. With you always
beside me I know that I will not falter.

Now you are sad, but I will see you again, and
your hearts will be filled with gladness, the
kind of gladness that no one can take away
from you.

—John 16:22

For many of us it is scary to think of surrendering ourselves into the arms of God. "What
might happen?" is the secret question that
pummels our thoughts. We do not yet fully
believe that God is *always*, yes always desiring
our good and our happiness. We do not yet
fully realize that God will be with us as a guiding power to love and sustain us through whatever hardships and heartaches life may bring.

—Joyce Rupp

I can remember when the thought of surrendering myself
to God was a frightening prospect. Somewhere in the
back of my mind was the thought that if I surrendered to
God I would be expected to accept whatever suffering
came my way, and I wasn't sure I wanted to volunteer for
any unknown suffering. As a result, I kept God slightly at
arm's length. I paid him the homage I considered his due
and tried to obey his commands to a certain extent, but a
part of me was reluctant to enter into a very deep relationship with him. Then when my world was torn apart by
grief and I really had nowhere else to turn, I began making my first tentative steps toward a relationship with him.
During that dark period when the wonders of this life no

longer held any delight for me, I felt myself start to lean into God, surrendering into him and feeling finally the comfort of his Love.

It was this surrender that freed me from fear. I grew to understand that God doesn't cause or send pain to us as a result of this surrender. Trials will come to us regardless of our relationship with our Creator. But in our surrender we are released from the bondage of our fearfulness. We are comforted by the knowledge of his Presence and love, and we are set free to experience our lives to the fullest, knowing that we are never left alone.

> *God of all creation, I surrender myself body and soul into your loving arms. I bless you for the freedom and the joy I feel in this act of surrender. You calm the fears and wipe away the tears of your children, and you protect us from the darkness of despair.*

Something is over. In the deepest levels of my existence something is finished, done. My life is divided into before and after.

—NICHOLAS WOLTERSTORFF, *LAMENT FOR A SON*

Several months before Andy died, Pat and I were having dinner with old high school friends. The younger brother of our friend had committed suicide many years before. Somehow our conversation got around to talking about the "good old days," and this long departed brother's name came up. Our friend got a far away look in his eyes talking of his brother and made this comment: "My life has been divided into two periods—before Rich and after Rich." How well I know now what our friend was talking about. The day Andy died has become a watershed date for me. Life will never be as it once was. This was a very painful fact for me to digest for a long time. I was very content with my life. I wasn't looking for change, particularly such a tragic change as the death of a child.

I remember resting upstairs in my bedroom the day after his death, while grieving family and friends gathered downstairs. When the phone rang, I considered letting someone else pick up, and then I changed my mind. However, before I could speak, I realized that a neighbor had already picked up the phone and was in conversation with another friend. I overheard the friend say to my neighbor, "They'll never be the same after this." I quietly hung up the phone and closed my eyes. The thought of never being the same again filled me with fear. I could feel the impending death of my old self, I feared it, and I didn't want to let go of the "before" part of my life.

However, as the months dragged by, I began to realize that a new person was indeed emerging, and coming to life. And I was surprised to find that I liked this new self even more than the old. I had not asked to be changed, but it had happened anyway. It was a painful and difficult birth, but my soul is more at peace with life than it was before. I am more alive spiritually, more compassionate, calmer. Little things don't send me into a frenzy the way they used to. I appreciate small things I didn't notice before. This, I believe, is one of the gifts given to those who mourn. Just as our loved ones are reborn into a new life at death, so we also can experience a rebirth of our spirits.

Father, guide my steps as a loving parent guides a toddler learning to walk for the first time. Help me to grow in compassion and love and faith, and keep me always beside you.

When the sultan asked the lad why he was in such haste the boy replied, "I just saw Death standing in the palace garden, and when he saw me, he stretched out his arms as if to threaten me. I must lose no time in escaping him." Agreeing, the sultan gave the boy his swiftest horse. When he left, the ruler angrily stalked into his garden and demanded to know of Death how he dared to intimidate the son of the sultan. Death listened, astonished, and answered, "I assure you, I did not threaten your son. I only threw up my arms in surprise at seeing him here, because I have a rendezvous with him tonight in Baghdad."

—HARRIET SCHIFF, *THE BEREAVED PARENT*

Everyone in our family and some of Andy's friends spent many sleepless nights making up "if only" sentences. We each took upon ourselves a measure of guilt and blame for Andy's death. "If only" sentences are so destructive. They will not bring your loved one back to you, and they serve no purpose other than to make your sorrow even more unbearable. The above passage in Schiff's book has, I'm sure, brought some measure of relief to countless bereaved parents who have read her book over the years. "If only" the young prince had not fled to Baghdad, would he have lived? How can we know the answer to these painful questions?

Many health care workers who work with accident and trauma victims are well aware of the fact that some people who should have had no hope of recovery have survived, and others who did not seem to be in danger have suddenly died. These professionals will be quick to attest to the belief that when it is our ordained time to die, we will die, and not before then.

Although at times it seems incomprehensible to us that our loved ones should have died when they did, it is

essential to our healing that we accept the fact that we all
are following a divine plan that we may not understand.
All of the "if onlys" are a part of that divine plan, a plan
conceived by a Father who yearns for our love and happiness and in whose ways we must trust.

Father, I believe that in your wisdom
you know what is necessary for us to
grow in love and to move closer to you.
Give me the faith to accept your will.

The soul would have no rainbow had the eyes
no tears.

—JOHN VANCE CHENEY

Today I was filled with a longing to hear the sound of
Andy's voice. I miss the sound of his laughter, his conversations with me, even the arguments we had, because all
of these were his sounds. The memory of it is fading, and
I never thought it would. I have lost something irreplace-
able, and today I mourn the loss of his voice. There are so
many things to mourn when someone we love has died:
their companionship, their love, their mere presence in the
world. We mourn because we are lonely for them, because
we miss them, because they were a part of our own lives.

After all of these months, I am learning how to handle
the feelings of loss when they overtake me. I relax into
them and I let myself miss Andy. I don't panic because
Sorrow is walking beside me today. I welcome her company
for a part of the journey, but I resolve that she will not lead
me along this path for long. She will merely accompany me
for a while and then she will allow lighter emotions to be
my companions for a time.

And I remind myself that each day of this journey called life, each step I take brings me that much closer to the journey's end. When that day comes I will once again hear the sound of my son's laughter.

> *Jesus, I know that in all my moments*
> *you are beside me. Sorrow will not*
> *weigh me down and fear will not slow*
> *my steps because you are my shepherd.*
> *It is only your voice that I shall hear.*

I wanted a perfect ending. Now I've learned, the hard way, that some poems don't rhyme, and some stories don't have a clear beginning, middle, and end.

—GILDA RADNER

What we see now is like a dim image in a mirror; then we shall see face-to-face. What I know now is only partial; then it will be complete—as complete as God's knowledge of me.

—1 CORINTHIANS 13:12

Outliving a child seems to defy nature. It felt so wrong to be alive when a child of mine was dead. One afternoon an old friend called to console me. He had lost two brothers to suicide during his life and was no stranger to the pain of loss. "I always planned to go before my children," I lamented to him. And he replied to me, "Well, that was your plan, not God's."

We don't know what our lives will bring. Sometimes we think we have utmost control over our destiny, our lives and future, and then tragedy steps in. A life is lost. An illness or injury disrupts our plans. Jobs and marriages end and our old goals and hopes are destroyed. We sometimes must accept the fact that, as much as we want to know the answers to all of our questions, there are some mysteries that we will not be able to solve in this lifetime. We may often ask the meaning of suffering, or why God chose to take a loved one from us, or why we must endure illness and loss. The only thing in this life that we can be certain of is that God does love us with all of his being. God is near us in the midst of all of life's unexpected tragedies, and he wants us to know his presence. We will not escape the sorrows of our lives, no matter how good, generous, or loving we are. Ultimately it is God, not we, who is in control of our destiny.

A basic tenet of our faith is the belief that some day we will have a more complete understanding of this life. If we accept the idea that there is a reason for every event in our lives, even events that bring us great suffering, then we can look forward with hope to the day of our understanding of life's mysteries. As we continue in this earthly life, if we search faithfully for understanding and answers to our questions, we will grow in wisdom and knowledge. This growth, I believe, is one of the reasons that we are put on this earth. The more we grow, the more fully we will live.

Lord, increase my faith. Let me be confident that you are always beside me. Teach me not to fear my future when you are beside me. Even though I do not always understand your ways, increase my faith in you that I may always be confident of your divine presence, guiding me along this pathway of life. Remind me often of your faithfulness, and let me remember that even though I do not

*understand all things, all of your
actions are grounded in your unending love for me.*

Your joy is your sorrow unmasked.
And the selfsame well from which your
Laughter rises was oftentimes filled with your
 tears.
And how else can it be?
The deeper that sorrow carves into your
Being, the more joy you can contain.

—KAHLIL GIBRAN

Sorrow carves a vast emptiness within us. In the early days of my mourning, I truly believed that I would never be happy again. I believed that laughter would never ring out in our home, there would be no more gatherings of friends, no more joy to be found in my life. I believed that I was destined only to live out each remaining day in despair and pain. While my sorrow was carving that emptiness within me, I felt that nothing mattered in this world anymore. There would be no more beauty or joy in my life. Little unimportant bothers no longer existed. Bigger worries could not capture my attention either. And when this vast emptiness had been opened up within me, I was surprised to notice that I was gradually allowing that void to become filled with things of beauty, laughter, joy, and delight in the day.

Just as a dentist's drill destroys the decay in an otherwise healthy tooth, the resulting hole is not left empty when the decay is cleaned out. The gap is filled with a substance that will strengthen the tooth and make it healthy again, not the same tooth as before, but a strong and healthy one nevertheless.

In a space in my soul where there was once nothing but pain, a loving God over time carved away the decay of my sorrow and filled my soul with a joy and a peace fired in strength. And this new joy is all the more delightful for having replaced the suffering that once occupied this space within me.

> *Father who heals our sorrows with his love, watch over us in times of despair. Let us know the nearness of you and lend us your strength. Comfort us who mourn and give us courage to live our lives with you as our center.*

Keep your face to the sunshine and you cannot see the shadow.

—Helen Keller

We must be optimistic during our days of mourning. We must believe that we will enjoy life to the fullest again some day. We must hold on to the belief that this heavy cloak of sorrow will not always cover us and weigh us down. We need to look for opportunities to celebrate. We need to reach out in the same way that flowers stretch and grow toward the sun. We are creatures of the light and we grow toward light. We were not meant to be in the darkness of grief and unhappiness forever.

While this time of sorrow is on us, we are in a period of dormancy, not death. We know that we must mourn for a while, that we must go into the darkness of our souls, but we believe that someday the sun will shine upon us again and we will stretch our arms toward the warm light of life.

Lord, be with me in this darkness. Even if I am unable to see you or feel your presence, increase my faith so that I may know that I am never alone or abandoned. Give me the strength to accept this time of darkness and grief, let me welcome the silence of my desolation, for it is in this silence that I will come to know you.

Time of Hope

Great religions promise that we will have company [at the hour of death]. Death related visions do, too. Hospice nurses tell story after story of dying patients reaching out with joy to someone unseen just before they die.

—MALLY COX-CHAPMAN, *THE CASE FOR HEAVEN*

I used to think that the Angel of Death would be a terrible thing. I realize now that the Angel of Death would have to be God's most tender and understanding angel, to be sent to us at such a significant, frightening moment.

—MARIANNE WILLIAMSON, *ILLUMINATA*

Angels are all the rage these days. You can hardly shop anywhere without finding something with an angel on it: candles, statues, dish towels, pictures, bookmarks, coffee mugs, and the list goes on. There are numerous books in print today about angels, everything from the history of these mystical beings to how to train your angel to respond when you call on them. I have a collection of angel items myself. I grew up praying the "Guardian Angel" prayer, and like many people, I take comfort in the idea that angels are around us.

But the cute image of angels being depicted commercially doesn't really mesh with scriptural accounts of angels, the messengers of God. Angels are not little invisible pets who hang around just waiting for our summonses. I believe these are powerful beings who constantly see the face of their Creator and who live to serve him.

I've never seen an Angel of Death on a dishtowel or a coffee mug, perhaps because the image most people would associate with such a being would be something resembling the Grim Reaper. But, as Marianne Williamson writes in her beautiful book *Illuminata,* the Angel of Death must be among the most beautiful and comforting of God's angels, an angel full of joy and excitement for the task of ushering God's precious children back home to him. How could the Angel of Death be a fearsome creature? If this messenger is to be our first glimpse of eternity, then it could not be anything other than breathtakingly beautiful.

What comfort then, to know that when our loved ones slipped away from our embrace, it was to fall into the arms of a being who emanated unimagined joy and love, and who carried our children, our parents, our friends straight into the arms of All Love.

> *Lord Jesus, you knew the presence of the angels during your own earthly ministry. We take comfort in believing that angels watch over us also, because we are the beloved children of their Creator. May we follow the example of the angels as we look always toward your Light.*

Not only were we told that the death experience was free of pain; people reported that they did not want to come back. After being met by loved ones, or guides, they traveled to a place that was so loving and comforting that they did not want to return.

—ELISABETH KÜBLER-ROSS, *THE WHEEL OF LIFE* (FROM INTERVIEWS WITH SURVIVORS OF NEAR DEATH EXPERIENCES)

Stories of near death experiences are becoming increasingly common these days. Some speculate that with advances in medicine and technology over the last few decades, many people who might have died in another age are being pulled back from the brink of death. These people are sometimes able to recount stories of traveling through a tunnel toward a source of Light and being surrounded by a feeling of great love and peace.

I remember returning home from the hospital on the day that Andy died. The house seemed to be full of people, and I walked out to the back yard where our parochial vicar, Father Jeff Goeckner, was sitting with my daughters. I sat down beside him and he put his arm around my shoulders while I cried. "Why did this happen?" I asked. "We prayed so hard." I'll never forget Father Jeff's answer to me. He gave me no platitudes about God's will, or the need to sacrifice, or the meaning of death. He knew I was angry with God. Instead, he just sighed and softly said, "Maybe Andy just got a little too close to heaven to want to come back." I could understand that. I could visualize my son being enveloped in a great blanket of love and warmth. I could imagine his overwhelming sense of peace and happiness, I could almost see his radiant smile and hear him saying, "This is where I belong. I'm here to stay. They'll be all right without me."

We, after all, are pilgrims bound for our true home. We wouldn't long so for it if it weren't a land of wonderful beauty and peace. There is thus a part of each of us that rejoices even in the midst of sorrow for our beloved who has reached the shores of our true home.

> *Lord, we are homesick for you. We, this pilgrim people, will never be content until we can finally reach the shores of the land you have promised us. Guide us each day on this journey, show us*

the path we must follow, and always walk before and beside us.

We sometimes congratulate ourselves at the moment of waking from a troubled dream: it may be so at the moment of death.

—NATHANIEL HAWTHORNE, JOURNAL, 10/25/1835

What a wonderful idea to think that at the moment of our death we should awake, look around, and realize that we are once again home where our spirits have longed to be for a lifetime. Maybe we'll look back at our time on earth and it will seem nothing more than a dream.

About a month after Andy's death, I was having a very difficult time. I desperately wanted a sign from God that Andy was safe. I needed to know where my son was. All weekend long I had prayed for a sign. It was a stormy weekend and I spent a lot of time staring up at the storm clouds as I begged God for a sign that Andy was okay. I didn't know what kind of sign I was looking for. I'd never before asked God for any kind of physical sign acknowledging that he heard me, so I didn't know what I expected. But as I spent long hours that weekend staring up into the stormy skies, I had an inkling that if I were going to receive some kind of message that my son was okay, it would probably come from the heavens.

On Monday morning, after receiving no sign of any kind that God had heard my prayer, I was at my lowest point, when suddenly the phone rang. It was my daughter Jill calling from school. I hadn't spoken to her for several days, so she was unaware of how badly I had been feeling. But in the middle of the morning she was overcome by drowsiness and went into her study room, lay down on the floor, and had a dream. In this dream, which she described as amazingly vivid, she could feel the wind blowing on her face as she and I stood in a field watching storm clouds gather. (As I had been doing all weekend, unbeknownst to her.) At some point I turned away from her, and when I did, the clouds parted and Jill beheld colors that were beyond description and in the sky she saw stars spelling out a message: "Hi, Mom, I'm Home!" In the dream she begs me to turn around, but when I do, the clouds close in again—and then Jill woke up. She immediately reached for the phone to tell me about her dream. "Mom," she insisted, "this dream was meant for you! The message I saw didn't say, 'Jill, tell Mom I'm home,' it was addressed to you, but you couldn't see it."

Her timing could have been nothing short of divine inspiration in light of the despair I had been feeling at that moment. When Jill repeated her dream to me, I felt a tremendous load lift from my soul. I truly believe that this was a message from Andy, a sign that I badly needed. And what could have been a more comforting message! My son was home! He was in a place of comfort, beauty, and joy. I could forever stop worrying about him.

> *Good Shepherd, bring each of us home at our appointed times. Keep those already with you close within your embrace and shower them with your divine love.*

As death, when we come to consider it closely, is the true goal of our existence, I have formed during the last few years such close relations with this best and truest friend of mankind, that his image is not only no longer terrifying to me, but is indeed very soothing and consoling! And I thank my God for graciously granting me the opportunity of learning that death is the key which unlocks the door to our true happiness.

—Wolfgang Amadeus Mozart

An old friend died this morning. The cancer that had invaded his lungs finally separated his soul from the sufferings of his body. I know his wife and children are grief-stricken. They were not ready to part with him. His brothers are devastated. I can imagine the shock and confusion they experienced in the hours after his passing and the heavy cloak of grief that will begin to settle upon them, a cloak that will only lighten itself as time passes.

But I also imagine Tim's soul soaring free and jubilantly away from his pain-wracked existence and into the waiting arms of his parents and loved ones who have gone ahead of him. I see him smiling down on his dear wife and small children, calling out to them, "Oh, if only you could know my joy! I am still here beside you, closer than you can imagine. I will never leave you. I will walk beside you forever. Your rejoicings I will share, your sorrows I will hold in my heart as I hold you."

While I grieve for the sorrow that his family endures at the physical separation they must experience, I rejoice for Tim, for his new life and for the peace and joy he has been awarded for all eternity. One day we will all celebrate together.

Divine Comforter, you gather the wounded and the suffering into your arms. You share in our sorrows, you weep and mourn with us, and you yearn to be our consolation. May those who mourn on this day find solace in your presence.

To die will be an awfully big adventure.

—James M. Barrie, *Peter Pan*

When I was about ten years old, my absolute favorite book was Barrie's *Peter Pan*. It was a book I read over and over again, both to myself and to others around me. This was during a time in my life when my parents were having marital and financial problems, we had moved several times, and our family life was in a general state of turmoil. I loved escaping with Peter, Wendy, and the Little Lost Boys to a land of fantasy and adventure, a land where boys and girls never had to grow up, where childhood could last forever. Yet, there was also a sense of longing among the children in Never-Never Land, a yearning to be loved, a need for a mother's warmth, a desire to grow and move on. This was something Peter Pan could never understand about his little tribe. He was content to remain forever in his land of make-believe. Growing up was the ultimate betrayal to Pan.

I think there are elements of both Peter Pan and the Lost Boys in each of us. We, on the one hand, want to grow and learn, to reach out and grasp all of life's experiences. Yet, on the other, we don't want to leave the safety of the world we know. The Peter Pan in us resists growth.

If we can look upon death as nothing more than an "awfully big adventure" we can take the sting out of it. We can recognize death as a part of our journey, not the end of our journey. If we can believe that there are wonderful worlds waiting for us on the other side of death's door, we can put aside our fears and learn to embrace each day as fully as possible. Our lives are more than a meaningless death march. There is no end, and death, when it comes, is nothing more than a big adventure, a stepping stone to a new life.

Lord, let me live each day as fully as I can. Let me take advantage of each

*day to grow in love and knowledge.
When it is time for you to bring me
home, let me be filled with wonder
and hope, and a sense of adventure.*

Jesus' going is unequivocally the end in terms
of everything they have so far seen. . . . Jesus
encourages them to grieve while they need
to . . . for He knows that it is only by walking
down that tunnel that they will come upon
and be surprised by the joy which lies ahead.

—NICHOLAS PETER HARVEY, *DEATH'S GIFT: CHAPTERS ON
RESURRECTION AND BEREAVEMENT*

Jesus never discouraged us from grieving the deaths of
our loved ones. He himself shed agonized tears at the
death of his friend, Lazarus, even though he knew that
within moments he would be summoning him back into
this world.

Even though we may believe wholeheartedly in the
promises of eternal life, we are still often overcome with
grief at the passing of our beloved. I imagine that the followers of Jesus had their moments of longing to be reunited with him, a yearning to once again see his smile or hear
his laughter. I'm sure that his mother missed the sound of
his footsteps or the feel of his face every day for the
remainder of her life.

Yet in spite of their mourning times, his friends and
family were a joy-filled, hopeful people, a group of men
and women who went gladly to their own deaths because
they knew without a shadow of a doubt that they would be
reunited with their Savior in the home of his Father. They
went to their deaths with this promise on their lips in the
hope that all people throughout the ages would hear their

words and know of this great and wonderful promise. And today we, their descendants, look beyond our grief with confidence in the truths spoken to us so many ages ago.

> *Lord, the promise of eternal life sustained your early followers during their times of grief and sorrow. They have passed down to us the good news of this promise, giving us also hope and strength in our darkest hours. Let us remember your promises when our hearts are burdened with the sorrows of the day.*

When you are sorrowful, look again in *your* heart—and you shall see that in truth you are weeping for that which has been your delight.

—KAHLIL GIBRAN, *THE PROPHET*

We wouldn't grieve the loss of someone who was insignificant to us. The fact that our grief is deep and our mourning is intense is a testament to the depth of the love we have held in our hearts for the deceased. However briefly we may have shared this life with our loved one who has gone on, this beloved person had brought wonderful delight into our lives. Our cry of sorrow is a song of love. When we acknowledge this, and accept the fact that love is eternal and undying, then we know that our relationship, bound by our love, will endure beyond any separation. And we know that no separation will be permanent.

Lord, we are all one in you. May we always keep in mind that our love for each other binds us for all eternity, with you and with those who live in you.

Sorrow is better than laughter; it may sadden your face, but it sharpens your understanding.

—ECCLESIASTES 7:3

Given a choice, I'd prefer a good laugh any day to a good cry. When I laugh deeply and completely, I feel a lightness of spirit, a peaceful happiness, and a feeling of relaxation.

Yet when I feel great sorrow, when I shed hot tears and cry out from the depths of my soul, I am more united with my brothers and sisters in this world. We are a suffering people. We all know tragedy in our lifetimes. Those who have suffered deeply and have learned from their pain are more capable of reaching out to others and helping them through their own hard times. They are more compassionate and empathetic. They will never be alone, because they have learned to reach out to those around them, both to those who are in need of comfort and those who can give comfort. When we look for and can find meaning in our suffering, when we are able to overcome our troubles and grow from our experiences, then we have been given a precious gift in this life.

Father, I offer my sufferings of the day to you. Use them to make me a better and more compassionate person. Help me to lead others who will walk this path out of the darkness of their pain.

One often calms one's grief by recounting it.
—PIERRE CORNEILLE

I remember sitting in my mother's living room on the night of Andy's funeral Mass. I was surrounded by caring friends and cocooned in a blanket of raw pain. When I look back on that awful night I remember repeating the story of the last week of Andy's life over and over again. Some of these friends needed no telling, for they had lived this week with me. For others, my story had been heard during the week, and some were hearing it for the first time from me.

I replayed in my mind and in my words the phone call, the rush to the scene of the accident, the conversation with the paramedics, the ride to the hospital. I repeated this story over and over again. I awoke each night for many nights and relived the horror of the memory of Andy's accident. With each repetition, the sense of horror lessened and became less foreign to me until it finally became a part of my history. In the retelling of my grief, it has become less frightening. My grief has assumed a familiarity and has become a part of me, no longer a fearsome entity, but a well-known companion. I no longer fear my grief, for it is not a stranger now.

Lord, you are always with me on this journey. You know my sorrows and my pain. You help me with the burdens I carry and calm my fears. May I always walk in your shadow.

Only with the appearance of the risen Jesus do the disciples see that God's ultimate word is love rather than condemnation. They realize what happened to Jesus [resurrection] is the destiny of all human beings.

—JON SOBRINO, *CHRISTOLOGY AT THE CROSSROADS*

Suffering and pain make little sense to me without God. . . . This does not mean that I have not prayed, as Jesus did, that it might be God's will that "this cup pass me by." But by embracing the pain, by looking into it and beyond it, I have come to see God's presence in even the worst situations.

—JOSEPH CARDINAL BERNARDIN, *THE GIFT OF PEACE*

I've read accounts of some of the great mystic saints of the Middle Ages who used to pray that God would heap afflictions upon them so that they might unite with him in his own suffering. Some of these holy men and women endured extreme physical and mental pain out of love for their Savior. I have never been one to volunteer for suffering. In fact, I'm quite fearful of any physical or emotional pain and can't imagine myself volunteering for any. It was not my idea to experience the pain of losing a child. For the first time in my life I could understand the desperation of Jesus on the night of his arrest as he pleaded with his Father in the garden: "Please don't make me do this. I don't know if I'm strong enough. I'm afraid." But finally, "Thy will be done." Jesus didn't suddenly change his mind about the suffering he was going to experience. He didn't lose the sense of terror that he felt at what was coming. But he accepted the will of God. St. Luke's Gospel tells us that at that point an angel came to strengthen him for the ordeal ahead.

God's angels are very near us during the lowest points in our lives. In your darkest hours you'll sometimes feel a soft breeze wafting across your face, cooling your spirit, or a slight lifting of the burden of sorrow for a tiny moment. You may feel a brief period of serenity in the midst of the turmoil of your grief, or a sense of sinking into a state of relaxation after a period of weeping. I think these are visits from the angels, sent by the God of suffering to strengthen us, the same way that they appeared to Jesus that night in the garden. They don't remove the cup of sorrow from us, but they give us the strength to drink it down.

Suffering Jesus, you drank the cup of sorrow with its bitter herbs of abandonment, desolation, fear, and betrayal. Like you, Lord, I want to turn away from this cup. I, too, am afraid and alone. Give me the strength to accept this burden and let the refrain of my mourning song be "Thy will be done."

He heals the broken-hearted and bandages up their wounds.

—Psalm 147:3

From the moment that the Creator first breathed a soul into a living being, we have had the capacity for heartbreak. When we read the ancient manuscripts of holy scripture, we realize that men and women from the beginning of our recorded time have endured the same sorrows and hardships that we encounter today. The heartbreaks of betrayal, loneliness, separation, illness, and death have been with us throughout our history, from the eras of primitive nomads until the present modern age. Throughout the ages humankind has realized that we are not alone in our pain. Many thousands of years ago the psalmist, a simple goatherder who became a king, reminded his people that God tended to his brokenhearted children and bound up their wounds.

How wonderful it is to just surrender our broken spirits into the healing hands of God, to rest our troubled hearts and minds and entrust ourselves to his care. Our faith in God allows us to be patient and trusting, as we believe that in his hands our wounds will be healed; our grief, our pain, our loneliness, all of our wounds will be tended to with love. With this faith, we can have no doubt that our Father will heal us in his own time, and once healing has occurred, we will be stronger and healthier than ever before.

> *Tender, healing God, I bring you all of my pain and sorrow of the day. I give my wounds to you, knowing that you will heal me and treat my wounds with the love of a mother whose child has stumbled and hurt herself. Your love will comfort me and heal me and you will make me strong in my faith and love.*

Suffering is a process of cleaning. The dirty linen goes through suffering in order to get clean. Would you call this suffering undesirable? Of course not. It has to go through this process in order to get clean. So those who are interested in getting cleaned should look for suffering. To burn. To purify.

—WILLIAM ELLIOTT, *TYING ROCKS TO CLOUDS: MEETINGS AND CONVERSATIONS WITH WISE AND SPIRITUAL PEOPLE,* INTERVIEW WITH SWAMI SATCHIDANANDA

> The edges of God are tragedy. The depths of God are joy, resurrection, life. Resurrection answers crucifixion; life answers death.
>
> —MARJORIE HEWITT SUCHOCKI

Today, as I write this, is Palm Sunday, or Passion Sunday. We are entering Holy Week, a week in which Christians focus on the suffering and death of Jesus. As Christians we are encouraged to look beyond the death of our Lord to his Resurrection, but during Holy Week we are reminded of the horrible sorrow and pain endured by Jesus on his journey into eternity. Sometimes, when a loved one has died, we spend a great deal of time re-living the suffering our loved ones might have endured during the final period of their lives. My son was thrown from a car and was never conscious after the accident, yet I spent hours and hours agonizing over whether he experienced any pain or fear during his last seconds of consciousness. I suffered many more hours than he possibly could have. The passion of Jesus should be a comforting reminder to us that the pain sometimes associated with death is but a fleeting moment before we burst forth into the awesome wonders of heaven.

Holy Week also reminds us that we do not suffer alone. Jesus has been there before us. He suffered the pain of loneliness when his friends deserted him, the pain of abandonment as he hung on the cross, the physical pain of the crucifixion, the pain of separation as he realized that he would be separated in death from those he loved. All of the emotions we experience in mourning were emotions he felt too. He suffered for us and reminds us that he knows what this pain is like. We can turn to him when we feel that no one else in the world understands our pain because he has suffered right beside us every moment.

Lord, you entered into this world to suffer every hurt that the human spirit experiences. Each time we hurt, you enter into our sorrow with us. You are always beside us helping us carry our own crosses. How could we make this journey without knowing you walk beside us? Remind me in my darkest hours of your suffering presence, and I will rest knowing I'm not alone.

We want you to know the truth about those who have died, so that you will not be sad, as are those who have no hope. We believe that Jesus died and rose again, and so we believe that God will take back with Jesus those who have died believing in him.

—1 THESSALONIANS 4:13-14

Our faith is one of our few consolations in times of mourning. Many times I have wondered how people who had no belief in an afterlife were possibly able to deal with the enormity of the death of a loved one. I don't know how I could continue on in this world thinking that Andy had ceased to exist. My belief in his continuing life was at times my only consolation and my only hope. Even if we go through periods of being angry with God for taking our beloved, we at least believe that our loved one was taken somewhere, that on some level he or she is still alive. Some of the New Age thinking offers slight comfort. Life after death is often portrayed as existing as an energy form in some vast void. I don't want that kind of existence for my son. Andy was and is so much more than a ball of light or an energy force.

The promises of Jesus sustain me in my lowest moments. Jesus promised his followers that he would take them home. He spoke of heaven as a place of peace and beauty and encouraged his followers to keep their eyes on their eternal goal. So convinced were these early disciples that they eagerly embraced martyrdom with a sense of hope and faith. Those who witnessed the deaths of these early martyrs in turn were convinced that their souls returned to the Father and Jesus. Many of the first century tombs bear evidence of this conviction. The promises of Jesus bring us hope in our darkest moments.

Source of Hope, let me always keep in mind your promise of eternal life, of a day when we will dwell forever with you and the Father. Comfort me with the assurance that my loved ones abide now with you in one of the places you have prepared for them, and keep my eyes on the road that leads me to your home.

Only faith in a life after death in a brighter world where dear ones will meet again—only that and the measured tramp of time can give consolation.

—WINSTON CHURCHILL, *MAXIMS AND REFLECTIONS*, 1947

When our world is beset by great catastrophes, many men and women struggle to believe in God. When war, famine, or natural disasters decimate entire families, villages, even countries, it is sometimes difficult to believe in the presence of an all-loving God. It is during such trying times that sometimes the only consolation to be had is faith in a better world beyond this one. Such faith often gets us through impossible grief and pain.

And as Churchill and so many others who have seen great suffering have assured us, "the measured tramp of time" will eventually soothe the rawness of our wounds. We are not unique in any of our hardships. Throughout the history of our civilization, men and women have endured every pain that we can imagine: the loss of loved ones, physical trials, emotional hardships, and eventually death. We are all one family in our suffering. We are comforted by others in our hard times, and in turn we extend our own hands in help when we are strong. Together, struggling, suffering, laboring in this life, we bring each other home. We are never alone.

Shepherd of all souls, keep your flock of lost and frightened sheep close to your side. Let us always hear your soothing voice when we are surrounded by darkness and are afraid that we've lost our way. Teach us to encourage and support our brothers and sisters on our journey, and lead us home.

No longer will the sun be your light by day or the moon be your light by night; I, the Lord, will be your eternal light; the light of my glory will shine on you. Your days of grief will come to an end.

—ISAIAH 60:19-20

The Bible is filled with passages reminding us over and over again that there will come a day when our sadness will end. This is such an encouraging message, repeated through the ages, since the time of humankind's first awareness of God's presence. God constantly reassures us that he will comfort us and care for us forever. In times of great sadness this is a wonderful consolation, this reminder that all of our sorrows will end one day and we will be filled with joy. Sometimes this message is the only comfort a grief-stricken person has. Our God has promised us for thousands of years that he will take away our sadness, and these words give us hope in our darkest hours.

> *Lord, I look forward with hope to the day of the fulfillment of your promises to me, and I give you thanks for the wonderful joy that my loved ones who have died to this life are now experiencing with you. May my prayers be united with theirs as we give you praise and as we wait for the day of our eternal reunion.*

A Christian who looks gloomy at the mention of death, still more, one who talks of his friends as if he had lost them, turns the bushel of his little-faith over the lamp of the Lord's light.

—George MacDonald

It is unrealistic to assume that, even if we have great faith in the promises of eternal life, we would not mourn the deaths of those who are dear to us. Those of us who have faith in eternal life do not mourn death as an ending, but as a separation. We mourn the separation that we must endure, but we do so as a hope-filled people. We live our expectation that death is not a forever parting, and this expectation gives us hope and comfort. We mourn because we miss those who have died, but even in our mourning we know that we will someday be together again. We grieve only for ourselves, for the sorrow that this separation brings to us, but we rejoice at the wonderful happiness that our loved ones are now experiencing.

> *Lord, increase my faith each day. Remind me each morning of my destiny as an eternal being, and help me to live each day as fully as possible, knowing that each moment brings its own unique gifts and opportunities to grow closer to you.*

Jesus declares that the disciples will have an abiding joy in consequence of his death, a joy in the light of which their immediate grief will be as nothing.

—NICHOLAS PETER HARVEY, *DEATH'S GIFT: CHAPTERS ON RESURRECTION AND BEREAVEMENT*

There are times when I sit and do nothing but think about Andy. I relive the horror of his death, I cry for the son I have lost, and I grieve because I miss him. There are moments when it seems that I've lost the energy to embrace the struggle that is this life, when living without my son is too great a burden, and I wonder how I manage to get up each morning and do the ordinary things that make up my day.

It is during these times of sorrow that I rely on the teachings of my faith. If I am to believe the words of Jesus, I know that this sorrow is but a temporary state. If I believe in his resurrection, then I must believe in my own resurrection to come, and I must rejoice that the promise has been fulfilled for Andy. If I truly believe in the promise of eternal life, then I know that my separation from all those whom I love is only for a short time. I am filled with hope that that which we call death is only a temporary parting.

Be with me, Lord, when I am worn out from my grief. Fill me with the hope of your promises. Let me remember that you have promised your followers great joy when the course of our earthly life is done. Let me be strengthened by that hope.

When you pass through deep waters, I will be with you; your troubles will not overwhelm you.

—Isaiah 43:2

It seems that all throughout Biblical history God continually reminded his people that he would not abandon them. He promised them time and time again that no matter what test they must face, no matter what hardship or trial came their way, he would be with them. He would keep them from harm.

There are times in our lives, especially in times of great tragedy or hardship, when we feel that God has abandoned us. When we are experiencing great trials it is often easy to feel abandoned and alone. Perhaps that is why God took such pains to continually remind his people that they weren't alone.

I remember being with my children in the swimming pool when they were young. At various times in their childhood each of them had moments of panic in the pool, when they were afraid of the depth of the water and began to flail about, and cry out for help. Usually I was right beside them, and all they needed to calm them was to hear my voice saying, "You're okay, I've got you," or to feel my arm around their waist. In their brief moments of panic in the deep water, though, they forgot that I was nearby; they didn't understand that I wouldn't let them drown in the deep water.

God feels the same way about us. Even when we are panicked and distraught, God is beside us. His arm is around us, and he is always reassuring us that he will not let us be harmed.

> *Lord, help me to keep in mind that you are never far from me. You will always protect me and keep me from harm. In moments of fear or despair, it is hard for me to remember these truths. Keep your promises in my mind.*

You live on earth only for a few short years which you call an incarnation, and then you leave your body as an outworn dress and go for refreshment to your home in the spirit.

—WHITE EAGLE

I believe that when you die you will enter immediately into another life. They who have gone before us are alive in one form of life and we in another.

—NORMAN VINCENT PEALE

The root cause of a man's grief and delusion is the identification of the Soul with the body. Fear of death paralyzes him because he is ignorant of the soul's true nature. The wise perform their duties in the world, cherishing always the knowledge of the Soul's deathlessness.

—SWAMI NIKHILANANDA, *PERSPECTIVES ON A TROUBLED DECADE*, EDITED BY BRYSON, FINKELSTEIN, AND MACIVER, 1950

Jesus said, "Now as for the dead rising to life: haven't you ever read what God has told you? He said, 'I am the God of Abraham, the God of Isaac, and the God of Jacob.' He is the God of the living, not of the dead." When the crowds heard this, they were amazed.

—MATTHEW 22:31-33

Life is real! Life is earnest!
And the grave is not its goal;
Dust thou art, to dust returnest,
Was not spoken of the soul.

—HENRY WADSWORTH LONGFELLOW, "A PSALM OF LIFE"

The prospect of reunion offers hope to bereaved parents that allows them the mindset to enjoy this life as a kind of way station until the joyous day when they will embrace their child again.

—JUDITH R. BERNSTEIN, *WHEN THE BOUGH BREAKS: FOREVER AFTER THE DEATH OF A SON OR DAUGHTER*

When Andy died, the idea of his ceasing to exist was an unthinkably painful thought. This energy that was my son, to whom I had given birth, had held and loved, could not possibly just one day become nonexistent. There had to be more to this life than what we could see. I had always believed in heaven, but it was more of an "I hope there's something else" than an actual knowing that there was an afterlife.

After Andy died, I began an almost frantic search for some evidence that some part of Andy was still out there. I spent many days asking God for a sign that he was okay. I wondered where Andy had gone. I knew his body was dead. I had held his lifeless hands. I had lain my tear-streaked face on his silent chest, and I walked with him to his final earthly resting place. Gradually, I began to know that Andy was more than his body. It was Andy's soul that I cried out for, that I worried about, and mourned. And in the searching, I found him.

It was only when I began to see the small signs that reassured me that he had indeed survived dying, that I knew in my heart that we are all eternal spiritual beings. I've felt his presence and seen signs of his continuing life. And I can believe these things because our Lord assured us long ago that our God is a God of the living. God did not say, "I used to be the God of Abraham. When Isaac was alive, I was his God too." He said, "I am the God of Abraham. . . . " He's speaking in the present tense. Abraham still lives with God. Jesus didn't tell us these things so that we could therefore stop worrying about Abraham's fate. He spoke these words to comfort and reassure us in our times of doubt and uncertainty, in our times of mourning and sorrow.

Death is tolerable only when we begin to truly believe that it doesn't really exist. Of course we can't deny the fact that our bodies eventually die. We who mourn have stood beside enough caskets to doubt that fact. But there comes a time when we know that the essence of who we are will not die. I will always miss his body, his beautiful blue eyes, his boisterous laugh, and the way his lips contorted when he tried not to smile. I miss his voice and his handsomeness. I miss all of him and know that, physically, he won't return. But I know that Andy is still with me, in my mind, my heart, and always in my soul.

> *Lord, you have promised us the gift of eternal life. We know that even though our bodies will die, we will rise again just as you did, and share eternity with you. In our times of sorrow, help us to remember that we are all eternal beings.*

The soul is not a physical entity, but instead refers to everything about us that is not physical—our values, memories, identity, sense of humor. Since the soul represents the parts of the human being that are not physical, it cannot get sick, it cannot die, it cannot disappear. In short, the soul is immortal.

—RABBI HAROLD KUSHNER

We know that the soul survives the body and that being set free from the bars of the body, it sees with clear gaze those things which before, dwelling in the body, it could not see.

—ST. AMBROSE (C. 340-397)

Life is the childhood of our immortality.

—JOHANN WOLFGANG VON GOETHE

In heaven, we do not lose, for "to die is to gain." We aren't less, we're more. When we die, we're not in some soul-sleep of a stupor, not purgatory, and we're certainly not unconscious. We are at home with the Lord. Home!

—JONI EARECKSON TADA, *HEAVEN: YOUR REAL HOME*

With the explosion of this century's advances in scientific knowledge, there are many scientists who today might proclaim that we know no such thing of the soul surviving the body. Something that cannot be measured or proven has no validity to the scientific mind. We have become a nation of skeptics. Just a few decades ago a popular theme was the idea that God himself was dead. But as we begin this new millennium, it seems that more and more people are turning once again to their spiritual roots. People are willing to acknowledge their beliefs in the survival of the soul, and I for one am glad to be a part of this generation.

I often need a reminder that I am a spiritual being. When sorrow threatens to swamp me, it is this reminder that buoys my sinking spirits. I need to remember that I am just a pilgrim in this land of suffering, it is not my home. Each step of my journey allows me to understand a little more clearly the purpose of the journey. I am here to grow in knowledge and faith, to learn to love and to know what it is like to be loved. I will endure hardships on this journey, and my knowledge of life and love will be stronger because of these struggles. As my spirit yearns for its own dwelling place, I can understand that sorrow is a fleeting emotion in my eternity, and that when I reach the end of this particular journey, I will come to a place where there will be no more tears.

There is no doubt in my mind that Andy is not dead, but set free. Although I will grieve for the loss of my son all of my life, a part of me rejoices for his sake. On the first anniversary of Andy's death I wrote a poem for him, part of which, copied below, expresses that very idea:

> But knowing that you're happy
> In a place you want to be
> And your earthly bonds are loosened
> And your soul is soaring free
> Gives me the strength to rise each dawn
> And put aside the dread
> And know you're walking with me
> Though you're just a step ahead.
> Your laughter echoes in the wind
> Your smile is in the sun
> And in the blinking of the stars
> We know your sense of fun.

Good Teacher, show me the paths of wisdom, patience, faith, and love, paths that will lead me closer to you. Walk beside me on this journey. Be my light in the darkness, my companion in the silence, my comfort in the desert. Protect me from the dangers of this journey, and at the end of the day, lead me to rest in your own dwelling place, when our earthly bonds are loosened.

Like many others before me, I have experienced "intimations of immortality." I can no more explain these than the brown seed can explain the flowering tree.

—Robert Hillyer, *This I Believe*, 1952

The experience of the immortal self does not come from education, conditioning, or science. The idea rises from the depths of your being and you quite simply know it to be true. Your invisible nature is real, yet we know also that it can never be surveyed and mapped. We know this because we can look beyond the dust of our bodies and in quiet, divine meditation experience immortality for ourselves.

—Wayne Dyer, *Wisdom of the Ages*

> If I err in the belief that the souls of men are
> immortal, I err gladly, and I do not wish to lose
> so delightful an error.
>
> —CICERO, *DE SENECTUTE,* C. 78 B.C.

No one has ever conclusively proven the fact of our immortality. Yet from the dawn of human consciousness, this is a concept that we have embraced. We instinctively feel the movements of our soul, we recognize its separateness from our human form, and we understand that the essence, which we call spirit, or soul, is eternal. It transcends human death. I have no way of proving that I am an eternal being. Neither do I have any way of proving my belief that God exists, or that those whom I love live on even after they have died. These beliefs are so firmly rooted in my being that there is no need for proof. It is, rather, a "knowing," an awareness, a feeling. There's an element of my being that transcends and rises above the existence of mere flesh and bones. This is my soul, my spirit, and the final essence of who I really am. This essence dwells for now along with my mortal body. I can't prove that this essence is separate from my physical self. In fact this soul of mine is very closely entwined with the physical part of me. But I know that one day this spirit will take flight from the physical dwelling, separate from this mortal life, and soar eagerly toward its eternal home. I cannot prove this. But I know the truth of it.

After the Vietnam War, as in other wars, many of our soldiers returned home missing arms and legs. I've often wondered how difficult it must be to adjust to life with a part of one's body missing. I've wondered how it must feel to be completely paralyzed, how awful the trapped feeling must be. Yet no physical accident can rob us of our souls. We can lose arms, legs, eyes, ears, breasts, tongues, and other organs, until only a small part of the body remains. Yet our soul is still complete. This is the part of us that is who we really are, the immortal part of ourselves that will not know death. At some level all of us know that there is infinitely more to the question of who we are than the mere composition of flesh and bones. We know that we are not our bodies, that our bodies are merely homes for our souls. We are eternal beings.

Sometimes I'm drawn into a discussion with those who don't believe in life after death. I hesitate to discuss my beliefs with these skeptics because I know that I have little chance of changing their beliefs and they have little chance of affecting my own beliefs. But one argument that I always maintain is this: We are all going to die one day. There is no argument about this fact. When I die, I will do one of two things. I will continue on into eternity and hopefully be reunited with those I have loved in this life. Or, I will cease to exist when I die. Either way, if I choose during this life to live with the belief in my eternity, then when I die I will not be disappointed. If I continue on into eternity, I won't be surprised, but if I merely cease to exist, I won't be around to be disappointed. On the other hand, if I live my life refusing to believe that I am eternal, then when I die, I again am faced with the same outcomes. Either I will be pleasantly surprised, or I will not. But what a life of hopelessness and despair I would have had in this lifetime if I had chosen not to believe in eternal life. What opportunities for growth and healing I would have missed if I had lived a life of disbelief. I choose to believe in my eternal self, and like Cicero, if I am wrong, I will have at least enjoyed a delightful error in this life.

Eternal Father, as your children, we will inherit your gift of eternal life. Let this belief be our comfort in times of sorrow and our hope in times of despair. Holy Spirit, be a source of enlightenment for me in this world. Open my eyes to the mysteries of life,

*and may I always be aware of your
presence surrounding me.*

The soul needs a physical body here . . . but
when . . . the body is no longer an adequate
instrument through which the soul may function, it lays the present body aside and continues to function through a more subtle one.

—ERNEST HOLMES, *THE SCIENCE OF MIND,* 1938

I can remember my elders telling me about my soul when
I was a very young child, the part of me that would go
to a place called heaven some day, the place where my
younger brother lived. I prayed each night "If I should die
before I wake, I pray the Lord my soul to take." I strug-
gled to imagine what a soul looked like, and somehow I
visualized little objects similar to California Raisin charac-
ters running around the heavens.

In my very young years my soul was like an internal
organ in my understanding, some vital part of me, but a
part whose function I was unsure of. It was only in my later
years that I came to understand that my soul is not just a
part of my being, it is my being. It is who I am and what I
am. The various parts of my body make up the sum of my
physical self, but if I were to lose an arm or a leg, or even
both arms and legs, my vision and hearing, and my mobility, I would still be a whole spiritual being. My body is not
who I am. I am my soul. It is my spirit that wants to experience a warm sunshine, or feel a raindrop. My spirit enjoys
great literature or beautiful music. Walking through a for-
est or along a seashore delights my spirit. Sunsets, starlight,
rainbows, flowers lift up my spirit. My body is the vehicle
that conveys the various sensations to my spirit. And when
my body ceases to function and dies, my spirit is freed from
its constraints and soars to its Creator. And I will be home.

Lord, my physical imperfections are not important to you. It is my soul that will stand before you one day. Guide me in this life that I will have the courage to mend my spiritual flaws and failings. May I listen to your words and work toward creating a clean and pure spirit in your image.

———— ∞ ————

If we've learned anything from the prophet Ezekiel and the apostle John, it's that heaven is real. It's not a state or condition, but a place. A place with streets, gates, walls and rivers. We are wrong in thinking that heaven is wispy, thin, and vaporous. It is earth that is like withering grass, not heaven.

—JONI EARECKSON TADA, *HEAVEN: YOUR REAL HOME*

Heaven became a real place to me only when my son departed for that land. I had professed all of my life to believe in the existence of heaven, but I had never known with an undeniable certainty of heaven's reality until Andy's death. Suddenly all the written words in bibles, theology books, and prayer books became clear. Heaven was not a metaphor or a hope. It was an actual state of being in which my son now dwelt along with other beloved relatives whom he had not met in this life.

It is a very real place, a place that is not far away beyond our galaxy, but a place that is as near as my next breath. My loved ones are close beside me as they watch over me and pray for me from their heavenly dwelling. I don't profess to know much about the makeup of that kingdom, what it looks like, how one occupies his time there, or how heavenly bodies or spirits appear to each other. These things are still delightful mysteries about which we can only speculate for now. But one thing I do believe now is that death does not remove our loved ones from our presence. Heaven is close by when we are united in love.

> *Lord of heaven and earth, there are so many things that I don't understand about this world and the one to come. Yet it is your will that as we live on this earth we are to grow in wisdom, knowledge, and love from all of our life experiences until we are ready to come to you. Open my mind and heart that I might live my life according to your will.*

There are two worlds, "the visible and the invisible" as the Creed speaks—the world we see and the world we do not see. And the world which we do not see as really exists as the world we do see.

—JOHN HENRY NEWMAN,
PAROCHIAL AND PLAIN SERMONS, IV, 1843

The day of death is when two worlds meet with a kiss: this world going out, the future world coming in.

—JOSE B. ABIN, *TALMUD J: YEBAMOT*, C. 400

The doctrine of the Kingdom of Heaven, which was the main teaching of Jesus, is certainly one of the most revolutionary doctrines that ever stirred and changed human thought.

—H. G. WELLS

If any one teaching of Jesus can be said to have given us the strength we need to face the trials of our lives, I believe it has to be his promise of eternal life in a home shared with a loving God. This is a promise that gives hope to those whose earthly lives are weighted down with sorrows and burdens. It's a promise that gives solace to those who are grieving the loss of a loved one. If we believe in this promise of Jesus, we will never feel that our lives are beyond hope. We will know that there will be a point at some time when all of our grieving, our suffering, and our tears will end. We look forward to a time of great celebration and joy.

Jesus, knowing that his followers were destined to live very difficult lives in the years after his ascension into heaven, consoled them over and over again with the promise of this eternal reward. The picture of heaven that Jesus painted for them, and his promises about the kingdom to come, gave those early followers the courage they needed to leave their homes and families, even to lay down their lives, in order to spread the wonderful news of this promise. Because of the faith and courage of these men and women, the promises of Jesus have been handed down through the ages to sustain and encourage us in our dark hours.

I wonder if I really believed in heaven before my son died. On the surface I know I did. I had been taught to believe in heaven from earliest childhood. But my idea of heaven was quite abstract, a dim, faraway place where a lot of resting peacefully was done in God's presence, where our memories of and ties to this earth were nearly nonexistent. Heaven was more a concept that I hoped was true than a concept that I really believed in. I wasn't particularly anxious to discover the truth about heaven for myself. I was more than content to live solely for today on this earth.

Andy's death has changed all of that. Like so many other parents who have endured the loss of a child, I have had all fear of death removed from me. I believe that this is one of the gifts we receive as a result of our mourning. I now know that heaven is real and that it is so much closer than I had ever imagined possible. Every Sunday I expressed my belief in the resurrection of the dead and the communion of saints without actually ever thinking about the words. Now, more than ever before, I know that I am an eternal being who will continue in life even after my body has died. I felt as if I had discovered some great and sacred truth, and was amazed when I began reading books on spirituality that these very beliefs are ancient and common. They are the beliefs I grew up being taught to profess without even thinking about them. What a great gift this awakening has been!

If we live our lives as if we truly believe the above quotes, then we live lives of confidence, hope, and courage. We know that we are eternal beings and that death is not a fearful enemy, but a passage to a life for which we have been destined, a life that our souls yearn for. Even though we grieve the loss of our loved ones who have left this world, we grieve the loss of their physical presence only. We know that they will be with us again one day when we ourselves enter our future home.

> *Father, do not let me be overcome with the sorrow of missing my departed loved ones. Keep alive in me the flame of faith that assures me of eternal life. Let me learn to rejoice for my loved ones who are celebrating that eternal life. Remind me that one day I too*

will know their bliss, and the tears
that I shed for them now will be forev-
er wiped away.

The body of a man is not a home, but an inn—
and that only briefly.

—SENECA, *EPISTULAE MORALES AD LUCILLIUM*, C. 63 A.D.

Our bodies are precious and miraculous gifts from our Creator. The more I learn about anatomy, the more amazed I am at the complexity and mystery of the human body. The human body is such a wonderful and miraculous machine, that there are many educated scientists who insist that there is no more to life than the body, that existence ceases with death.

I believe that as precious and valuable as our bodies may be, our souls are amazing beyond our poor imagination. We can only wonder at the power and glory of our immortal souls when they are released from the confines of these earthly bodies. Sometimes I wonder what God must have intended for our souls when he chose to clothe them for a period of time inside a cloak of humanness. Perhaps our souls feel like we might when we have an arm or a leg encased in a plaster cast for a length of time. The purpose of the cast is to heal an injured limb and to limit its mobility while the healing and growth are taking place. When the healing process is finished and the cast removed, our arms or legs feel wonderfully weightless and free. We may not be quite comfortable with this new freedom at first, but as we move around for a while without the cumbersome cast, we wonder how we ever tolerated the device as long as we did. The cast itself is not a part of who we really are. It is merely a healing device. Perhaps our bodies serve the same purpose for our souls. With the garment of the human body we learn and grow and heal toward the Creator. And when our growth is complete, our spirits break out of their earthly bonds and soar eagerly toward home.

> *Father, my soul remembers no other home than the body I now inhabit. I thank you for this precious gift of humanness. May I take care of my body out of respect for this gift of yours. When my life on this earth is finished, guide me toward your Light.*

> When I am dead, come to me at my grave,
> And the more often the better. . . .
> As you spoke to me when I was alive, do so
>   now,
> For I am living, and I shall be forever.
>
> —St. Serafim of Sarov

I talk to my son all the time. In the beginning, I often shouted at him for dying and for hurting all of us, but I have forgiven him now. I tell him how much I love him and miss him. I ask him to pray for us, especially his brother and sisters when they are driving. I talk to him wherever I happen to be: in the car, at the cemetery, at the kitchen sink, in church, wherever. I feel a connection to him that can never be broken, and I know that he is always with me. Death has forever severed the physical bonds between us, but the spiritual beings that we are will always be bound together.

I pity those who do not have this sense of connection. Their grieving is so much harder, their desolation so much greater, it seems to me. In talking to bereaved people who have lost hope, who have given up on God, there is often a sense of anger and bitterness that drives them, that denies them solace and slows their recovery. I feel blessed to have this belief in everlasting life. It is a great comfort to me. It gives me the strength to get up each day, knowing that this is only a partial separation and only for a short time, and then we will be together again. It's a great comfort to know that we aren't alone in this universe, that all of those whom we loved in this life and who have gone on are still present to us, still involved with our joys and our sorrows.

> *Lord, I believe in your promise of everlasting life. I look forward to the day when your promise to me shall be fulfilled. With the comfort of that belief I have the strength to awaken each morning and see the beauty of the creation you have prepared for me, and I thank you for the gift of each new morning.*

When somebody you love has died, the barrier between these two worlds grows very thin, and a new pattern of events is set free to happen around us.

—Nicholas Peter Harvey, quoting Stephen Verney,
Death's Gift: Chapters on Resurrection and Bereavement

In the past year and a half I have had the opportunity to share my feelings of bereavement with several other people who also have lost loved ones. Almost without exception, these people from many different walks in life and many different ages or creeds have experienced some sort of communion with a departed loved one. I personally know five people who have actually seen and spoken to a deceased relative. In four of these cases the deceased was a parent. In the other, a brother appeared to a sister. I was amazed at the number of people who were close to me who were able to share such astounding stories. Yet, they told these stories to very few others, perhaps out of fear of being thought delusional or unstable. I wonder how many others have seen a loved one but are hesitant to discuss it with anyone who might be skeptical.

Last year I attended a National Bereaved Parents Conference. One of the featured speakers was Judy Guggenheim, who co-authored Hello From Heaven!, a book that details accounts of spontaneous ADCs, or "after death communications." Ms. Guggenheim's presentation was the most heavily attended of all the sessions, and nearly every parent in the room was eager to share with the rest of us some ADCs that they themselves had experienced.

After Andy's death, I felt somehow that I was very close to a spiritual realm. I felt that this realm, heaven as I've always known it, was very near by, not some distant shore as I'd previously thought. It seems that when someone we love dies, a part of us passes through the veil that separates the two worlds. We are able to feel a closeness with the person who has died, and we realize that heaven might not be as far away as we had once believed. This was as close to being comforted as I could experience in the early days of my grief. It eventually helped to ease the pain of separation by enabling me to believe that my son still lived even though on a different level, a level that was not far from me after all.

Jesus, over and over again you soothed the troubled minds of your disciples with the promise of eternal life. So firm was their belief in your promises that they were willing to give up their earthly lives in order to spread your word to all people down through the ages. With faith in your word, we believe that our loved ones are already living in eternity with you and sharing in your joy. We rejoice for them even as we mourn their physical separation from us. We wait and hope for the day when we too will enter your kingdom and be reunited with those who have gone before us.

I'm aware that people I have loved and have died and are in the spirit world look after me.

—DIANA, PRINCESS OF WALES

My sister and I often find dimes on significant occasions or in unusual places. We tell each other that these are signs from Andy. We also watch out for the number 7, the day of his birth. I remember the night my sister's granddaughter Madolyne was born, several weeks before her due date. This is a little girl my sister has waited most of her life to meet, having had no daughters of her own. When her son and daughter-in-law called her to come to get their two-year-old son so they could leave for the hospital, she stopped quickly at the store on her way. As she was making her purchase, the cashier looked apologetically at her and said, "I hope you don't mind, this is the only change I have," and with that, handed her seven dimes! It was obvious to us that Andy was letting us know that he was joining in the excitement of his little cousin's arrival in this world.

I firmly believe that our loved ones are intimately involved in our triumphs and sorrows. Although we are not privileged to share in the mysteries of their heavenly existence, we are still in communion with them, a belief we attest to each time we profess our belief in the communion of saints in the Apostles' Creed. During times of deep depression, I feel Andy drawing close to me for the short time it takes to reassure me of his love, and then he's off again just as quickly as he was in this life. Sometimes, it's easy to believe that he's only stepped into another room, away from my sight, but always within hearing distance.

> *Lord, you promised each of us ever- lasting life. We thank you for the gift of eternity that our loved ones who have gone before us are now enjoying. We look forward to our reunions with them, and we try to keep in mind the many blessings you have already bestowed upon us in this world. For all of these gifts we thank you.*

[Those who have lost children] know for a fact that our children often return to us in dreams. This is not goofy, wild-eyed, wishful thinking. . . . It's fact. Sometimes I think they come to check in on us, to see how we're doing. More often they come to let us know how they're doing.

—Elizabeth Mehren, *After the Darkest Hour the Sun Will Shine Again*

What if you slept?
And what if,
In your sleep
You dreamed?
And what if,
In your dream,
You went to heaven
And there plucked
A strange and
Beautiful flower?
And what if,
When you awoke,
You had the flower
In your hand?

—SAMUEL TAYLOR COLERIDGE

Six weeks after his death my father appeared to
me in a dream. . . . It was an unforgettable
experience and it forced me for the first time to
think about life after death.

—CARL JUNG (QUOTE FROM *MEMORIES, DREAMS,
REFLECTIONS*)

Many bereaved people speak of dream visits from their
loved ones, dreams that seem to be much more than
an ordinary dream. Scripture is filled with accounts of mes-
sages given in dreams. Many modern-day books on
bereavement or life after death include accounts of dream
visits. I haven't been fortunate enough to have such a
dream, even though I would welcome one. But many of
Andy's relatives and friends have shared dreams that they
have had in which Andy seemed to be with them.

A few days after Andy's funeral, my daughter Jill shared
a dream she had had the night before. In it she was sitting
on a swing overlooking a meadow, and she was crying.
When she looked over she saw Andy sitting on the swing

beside her. He asked her why she was crying, and she replied that she was crying because he had died. Andy laughed and said, "I'm right here. I'll always be right beside you." As the dream continued, Jill and Andy laughed and ran through the field and, in the way of dreams, they became different ages as they played.

Several of his friends wrote me from their schools telling me how a dream of Andy helped them cope with the loss of his presence. In most of them he seemed to be telling them that he was okay, and not to worry about him.

Who can ever know whether such happenings are the work of wishful thinking or actual visits from a loved one? From the testimony of people who have had such dreams, there seems to be no doubt in their minds that these experiences are more vivid and realistic than ordinary dreams. Most people feel a great sense of peace after waking from such an encounter. Whatever the source of such a happening, I have no doubt that these are little gifts of comfort from God. Who else is the Giver of peace and comfort? I would welcome a dream visit from my son. I look forward to that possibility some day, and until that time should come, if it ever does, I trust that all things happen according to God's plan and according to his timetable.

Lord, you often use dreams to comfort and heal us or to warn us of possible danger. Dreaming is another form of praying as if, as we should do when we pray, we are listening for your word. Whether I am awake or asleep, Lord, let me always have a place of stillness within me that is listening for your whisperings.

I don't know what happens after death, but I know there is an after. I know what the process of dying is. I can tell you what the first earthly half-hour is. [laughter] But I don't know what goes on after, because I haven't been there.

—WILLIAM ELLIOTT, *TYING ROCKS TO CLOUDS: MEETINGS AND CONVERSATIONS WITH WISE AND SPIRITUAL PEOPLE,* INTERVIEW WITH STEPHEN LEVINE

In the past few years I've been interested in the stories of those who claim to have had near death experiences. A part of this fascination is my desire to catch a glimpse of the Home that my son now lives in. Most people who believe they have had an NDE speak of being drawn through a tunnel and into a radiant light where a Being of Light engulfs them in unconditional love. Many of these people told stories of having been met by departed relatives, loved ones, or religious figures. At some point in the experience they were told that they must return to their bodies, that their time had not yet come to leave this life, and many people expressed great disappointment at having to return to their bodies. Almost all of these people stated that as a result of their experience, they no longer feared death.

These stories are comforting and wonderful to hear, but we will never be completely sure of their accuracy until we each undergo our own death. In the meantime, if we believe in the promises of Jesus and of the many holy people of different religions, we can continue our lives in the conviction that our loved ones, and one day we too, will fully experience the wonders that eternal life holds for us.

Heavenly Father, we have faith in the promises your Son gave us. We believe in the coming of your kingdom in heaven, and we ask that you shower

your love on those who have gone home
to be with you forever.

Going to heaven!
I don't know when,
Pray do not ask me how, -
Indeed I'm too astonished
To think of answering you!
Going to heaven!
How dim it sounds!
And yet it will be done
As sure as flocks go home at night
Unto the shepherd's arm!

—EMILY DICKINSON

If we believe that one day we will be "going to heaven," as Emily Dickinson puts it, we have no room in our lives for hopelessness. We know that all things in this life—good things as well as sorrowful things—are temporary conditions. No tragedy in this life, and no great good fortune either, will prevent us from some day entering into a state of joy that will be unending if we manage to hang on to our faith.

We should always be mindful of the fact that we are merely pilgrims in this land, and the ups and downs of our lives are nothing more than parts of our journey. Sorrow does not have the power to overwhelm us, even though it may bring us to our knees sometimes. Happiness, by the same token, is merely a gift on loan, a dim foreshadowing of the even greater bliss of the next world. We are a hope-filled people. We have faith that a day will come when all of these earthly burdens will be laid down and we will end our wanderings. If we believe this, then the worries of the day will have no power over us.

Lord, I believe that some day I will be united with you for all eternity. Let me live each day of my life in joyful anticipation of that wonderful home-coming. And until that time may I live each day as fully as it is in my power to do. May all of my thoughts and actions be prayers of praise and thanksgiving for this great gift of life.

The only way you can go through this is by not relying on your own strength which you know intuitively is inadequate, but by knowing that God is with you in this. . . . If I thought for whatever obscure, complicated, ultimate reason God was doing this, I don't think I could have tolerated that. But to know that God was on my side, I could continue to turn to Him for strength because He wasn't the perpetrator.
—RABBI HAROLD KUSHNER, QUOTE FROM *TRANSCENDING LOSS* BY ASHLEY DAVIS PREND

Trust in the Lord with all your heart, and do not rely on your own insight.
—PROVERBS 3:5 (NRSV)

God continues to love us, even when we are angry at Him.
—JAMES DOBSON, *WHEN GOD DOESN'T MAKE SENSE*

I was very angry with God when Andy died. I didn't lose my faith, thankfully, but I did lose my trust. I had trusted that God would keep my children safe from harm in light of the many prayers for their safety that I had sent his way from the moment each of them had been born. I still struggle a little bit with the issue of trust. I cannot trust that God will deliver my children from earthly harm. I can't trust that we won't suffer illness or financial ruin or betrayal by loved ones. I can't trust that my marriage will last until death, or that my parents will enjoy their old age and not be a burden to their children. I can't trust that my three surviving children will be spared the heartaches of life. In a sense, I don't trust God the way I once did.

But I love God more fully. I believe in God more deeply. I realize that my trust was misplaced. God never promised to deliver us from the sufferings we were meant to encounter in this life. He only promised to help us through it, to love us and to bring us home. I am so thankful that I didn't lose my faith when Andy died. I would never have been able to face the loss of him if I had no belief in God's plan for us. There would be no hope left for me. And I thank God that he allowed my anger and my loss of trust, and let me feel his compassion and love. It sustains me from day to day.

> *God, Father and Mother, you are ever faithful to us, even when we turn from you. You accept our anger and our hurts, and you constantly stretch forth your hands to hold us, comfort us, and heal us. Let me follow your example today as I try to be more understanding of those in my life who are also hurting.*

Jesus did not promise to take away our burdens. He promised to help us carry them. And
if we let go of ourselves—and our own
resources—and allow the Lord to help us, we
will be able to see death not as an enemy or a
threat, but as a friend.

—JOSEPH CARDINAL BERNARDIN, *THE GIFT OF PEACE*

Frank Moody was a wonderful man. The father of a
large family, he was loved by everyone who knew him.
He had an Irish twinkle in his eyes and a cheery greeting
for everyone he met. He had nicknames for just about
every kid he knew. His youngest son Matt is one of my son
Sean's oldest friends. Frank delighted in the antics of our
boys and seemed to enjoy life to the fullest. Then one day
he learned that he was losing a battle with cancer and his
time on this earth was coming to a close. Sean and Andy,
along with the rest of us, watched with disbelief as the once
vibrant man became more and more frail physically, but
without relinquishing his sunny cheerful manner. He
would still call out his greeting to Andy, "Hey, McGiffer,
how are you today?"

One day my husband Pat was visiting someone at the
hospital when he ran into Frank at the coffee shop and they
sat down to share a cup of coffee. As they chatted, Frank
began talking to Pat about his impending death. And
Frank, with a rare expression of seriousness on his face, said
to Pat, "Paddy, the last time I went in for surgery,
Someone was right beside me, right at my shoulder, and I
felt absolutely no fear. I know I'm dying, and I'm looking
forward to it. I don't have the least fear of it in the world,
for I know I'll be taken care of all along the way." Frank
had learned to surrender to God's will, and as a result,
death was not an enemy to Frank. He met death with the
same cheerfulness with which he met everyone with whom
he came into contact. On October 31, Frank was near

death. His family prayed for only one thing: that he live past midnight, for Frank hated Halloween and they didn't want to say goodbye to him on a day he had always disliked. And Death, having befriended Frank, waited until a few minutes past midnight and took him home on All Saints' Day.

Andy's grave is one row from Frank's. One day after Andy had died, Matt and Sean were together and Matt shared a memory of Andy. At Frank's funeral, Andy had come up to Matt and offered his sympathy. He said to Matt, "Your dad's the first friend I've ever had die." Matt was touched that Andy, the "kid brother" he'd known all his life, had considered his dad a friend. It's often said that when we die, loved ones who have gone before us come to greet us. I just know that Frank was at the gates waving to Andy with a cheery, "Let's go, McGiff! We've got a baseball game to see!"

> *Lord, be with us at the hour of our death. Release us from our fears and fill us with peace. Remind us of your promises to us. Watch over our loved ones who rejoice now with you.*

God gathers our pain and struggle and holds it compassionately. It is good to bring God our tears. God can catch them and hold them compassionately until we find our inner peace again.

—JOYCE RUPP, *THE CUP OF OUR LIFE*

> We must believe that the Lord loves us, embraces us, never abandons us (especially in our most difficult moments). This is what gives us hope in the midst of life's sufferings and chaos.
>
> —Joseph Cardinal Bernardin, *The Gift of Peace*

Last night I had an unsettling dream. In this dream Andy was about eighteen years old, the age that he was when he died, and I had just learned that he had an illness that would take his life in five years. He would gradually grow weaker and weaker, and I would watch him die all over again.

The pain in this dream carried over into my waking hours. There was a Mass in remembrance of Andy that morning, and as I sat in church waiting for Mass to begin I closed my eyes and tried to clear my mind to find some peace, but the disturbing feelings of the dream kept intruding. So I visualized placing the burden of this dream in a bag and handing it over to Jesus, saying, "I give my pain to you."

It's a very releasing feeling to turn one's burdens over to God, and usually I feel a sense of relaxation after doing this. But today I imagined that I heard Jesus whispering to me, "It's really not that big a burden. Why don't you see if you can carry it yourself for a while. There's a hole at the bottom of the sack and your sorrow will trickle out of the hole during the day until you have released it all."

And so I visualized the hurts seeping out of the bag like grains of sand during the day. By the end of the day, as a result of thinking about my dream of the night before, I had gained a new understanding of those who suffer anticipatory grief, the grief of watching a loved one die slowly. I experienced that feeling in my dream and in my reflection of the dream during the day. I learned that anticipatory grief is a very difficult and painful journey that some are called to take. It was a lesson in compassion for me. I feel that this dream was given to me, not to cause me more grief over my son's death, but to enable me to reach out to others who are grieving with renewed compassion and understanding. When I reach out to others, it is Christ in me reaching out his own hands through me. And when I am in pain I will always feel his arms around me through the caring of others.

> *Good Shepherd, the more I come to know you the more secure and peace-filled I become. Your presence is strengthening and soothing, your love binds all our wounds. Never let me lose sight of you.*

He heals the broken-hearted and bandages their wounds. He has decided the number of the stars and calls each one by name.

—Psalm 147:3-4

Recently we spent the afternoon on a friend's house-boat. As evening settled in and the sky darkened, our friend brought out a night vision scope that his daughters had given him for his birthday. We all took turns playing with it, marveling at how clearly we could see the nearby shore. When it was my turn to look through the scope, I aimed it toward the heavens and was awestruck at what I saw. The sky was bursting with stars, more stars than I had ever imagined. When I looked at the sky with my naked eyes, I was able to see only a few stars, nowhere close to the huge amount of stars visible with the nightscope. The lights of the nearby towns and the pollution we've created have managed to blind us to one of the most startlingly beautiful sights of our universe.

I realized once again that there is so much in our world that we cannot see or understand. There are many mysteries right before us all the time, but sometimes we are unequipped to observe them. God's light is like the light of the stars I saw on that night. It is a brilliant, powerful, eternal light. It is always present to us, but we have been blinded from his light by the artificial light and pollution that we create all around us. It is in times of sorrow or hardship, when our souls enter that dark night of pain, that we are at last able to see the wonderful, mysterious light of God's love, a love that, like the stars above us, is there all the time, just waiting for us to behold it.

Father, never let me forget that you are always beside me. Remind me today that even if I don't always acknowledge your presence, you are nevertheless beside me. In you alone will I find peace and comfort.

No man dies before his hour. The time you leave behind was no more yours than that which was before your birth, and concerneth you no more.

—MICHEL DE MONTAIGNE, *ESSAYS*, XIX, 1580

I know that the Highest of High has a plan. I know that He has a time for me that will be right for me to leave my body the way a butterfly leaves its cocoon. Our only purpose in life is growth. There are no accidents.

—ELISABETH KÜBLER-ROSS, *THE WHEEL OF LIFE*

Physical life always has purpose and meaning. It is intended to be a spiritual learning experience, an opportunity for change, personal growth, and transformation for each of us. . . . Death is merely the final stage of physical life when we have completed our earthly school, cast off our body, and graduated. The assurance of an afterlife . . . can inspire us to overcome our fear of death so that we may be free to embrace life spontaneously and joyously.

—BILL GUGGENHEIM AND JUDY GUGGENHEIM,
HELLO FROM HEAVEN!

D r. Elisabeth Kübler-Ross has taught many lessons on the sanctity of life and the need to believe that we live out our lives on this earth in accordance with God's plan. According to Dr. Kübler-Ross, everything that happens to us happens for a reason, and each occurrence is meant to teach us. In the opinion of Dr. Kübler-Ross and many other like-minded individuals, we are all put on this earth to learn what is necessary for our growth and then we "graduate" back to our home in heaven. Some people learn the lessons they came to learn in a few short hours. Others need many decades to complete their learning. No one dies before his or her appointed time.

Sometimes we who are left grieve because we feel that our time with a particular person was too short. Other times we are saddened because someone we love is trapped in a body many years beyond the time they would have chosen to leave. Although we may not at this point understand why these things are so, I believe that when our own journey is completed and our eyes are opened, everything will finally make sense. Until then it is our task to grow as fully as we can in wisdom and knowledge and love. We need to help each other in our times of need, to forgive each other the hurts we inflict, to comfort each other in times of sorrow, to share in each other's joy and good fortune without envy, and to live each day as fully and productively as possible. We may not understand many of the tragedies that befall us in our lives, but if we look and listen closely during those hard times, we will learn the lessons that were meant to be taught and we will grow from that knowledge. Each lesson that we learn brings us one step closer to what Dr. Kübler-Ross calls "graduation," that time when we are called to return home.

When a person loses his fear of death, he is able to fully partake of this earthly experience. A man or woman who truly believes in the continuity of life is released from bondage to this earth. We become aware of the great gifts that belong to us in this life, and we welcome any opportunity to grow in knowledge and wisdom. We form a deep appreciation of the beauty of this world, but we are not fearful of our eventual and inevitable separation from this human existence. We are confident that the wonders of life will continue into eternity. Thus, we become a hope-filled people. As a people filled with hope, we are eager to experience all that this world has to offer us. Our sorrows and trials become our challenges and tests, but we know that they will not overcome us. We know that all things must pass away on the road to eternity, and we understand that no pain will have permanent claim on our hearts and souls.

Our prayers during our season of grief must also include hymns of thanksgiving for the enlightenment given to us during our times of grief, and for the awareness of the Divine in our lives, an awareness we might not otherwise have reached in better circumstances.

Father, I don't always understand your ways. Sometimes I question my own purpose in this life. Give me the courage to trust that you are with me in all things. Remind me to live my

*life by following the example of your
Son who taught us that above all
things love for you and for each other
is the most important. When my work
is done, welcome me into your light as
one of your faithful children.*

I would never say that my brother's death was
a blessing, but I can now say that the insights
and spiritual growth that eventually came out
of that experience were blessings disguised
within the sorrow.

—JOYCE RUPP, THE CUP OF OUR LIFE

In the months after Andy died I told many people that I
had felt a sense of giftedness, a feeling that in my grief I
had been somehow blessed. Once at a bereavement group
I ventured this opinion and an elderly widower questioned
me about that statement. "How can you say that?" he
asked. "What is blessed about this awful loss?" At the time
I had difficulty explaining that feeling. I didn't by any
means consider Andy's death to be a blessing, but in some
way I felt the beginnings of some sort of awakening that I
could not really explain. I felt blessed to have had my faith
strengthened instead of destroyed by this catastrophic loss.
I was blessed to have learned how deeply God loves me,
how intimately involved he is with each moment of my life,
and how fully present he is at any moment I choose to listen for him.

I was gifted to learn how good people are, how priceless
friendship is, how comforting the compassion of others can
be. I received the gift of a renewed thirst for knowledge, a
need to know and understand more about the workings of
this universe, a desire to express my creativity, and an urge

to give back to others who are in need. These are the gifts of loss. They do not compensate for the loss, but they help us to bear the burden and to strengthen our souls.

> *Lord, you beckoned us to come to you with our burdens and receive rest from you. You strengthen and console us with your love. Let us never be parted from you.*

We noted four kinds of changes in [bereaved] parents' attitudes toward death. The first, wanting to die, is a very transient reaction to intolerable pain. The remaining three attitude changes are enduring. These three altered perspectives suggest: (a) that death loses its usual macabre overtones; (b) that death brings the welcome prospect of reunion; and (c) parents see subsequent death very differently forever after.

—JUDITH R. BERNSTEIN, *WHEN THE BOUGH BREAKS: FOREVER AFTER THE DEATH OF A SON OR DAUGHTER*

I recognized my own feelings in the above quote from Judith Bernstein. In the first few months after Andy's death I couldn't imagine that life would ever again hold any joy for me. I felt as if my own life had ended with his death, and my remaining days on this earth would be marked by sadness and the passing of each day until death would finally relieve me of this pain. In the midst of this pain, death began to take on a different look in my mind. No longer a thing to be dreaded, death was instead something to be anticipated, a surceasing of this tremendous pain. I also began to realize that with my death I would be reunited with my beloved son, and death lost its power to frighten me.

Now I feel differently about death, just as Bernstein states. I pity those who live in fear of death. They are not yet convinced of the reality of the continuation of life. One of the gifts I have received in the wake of this great loss is that the fear of dying has been taken from me. This in turn has freed me to live my life more completely and confidently, with less sense of futility and despair. I no longer yearn for my own death. My life has become bearable once again, and, in addition, my future looks brighter than it did before. For I know now that all of my hopes and feelings and loves will not die with my earthly body, but will accompany me into eternity.

> *Father, you sent us your Son to conquer death and reveal to us your love and your desire to share your eternal home with us. We thank you for revealing these truths to us, for they give us courage and hope on the journey.*

It is only after [Jesus'] death that His friends will be able to recognize who He is. There is here an exact parallel with the evidence of many bereaved people that it is only after the beloved's death that he or she is perceived in his or her true stature. . . .

—Nicholas Peter Harvey, *Death's Gift: Chapters on Resurrection and Bereavement*

My mother is often amused and sometimes slightly exasperated when people begin to canonize their loved ones who have died. She claims that she can't understand how people manage to remember only the best qualities of those that have died and speak of them as if they had been living saints. I read somewhere that this is because only the best of people's qualities survive with them when they reach heaven's shores. Their weaknesses and faults are buried with their physical bodies. We had a friend who left his wife of nearly twenty-five years for a woman who was his daughter's age. During the few years he was married to this young woman, his old friends wanted nothing to do with him. Then he died very suddenly, and now we find ourselves missing our old friend and reminiscing about him in ways that we had not done in the last years of his life. We were able to recall and treasure the good memories of our friend, even though that friendship had ended before his death. Those things we had rejected in him now seemed so much less important.

When Andy died, I was able to look at the entirety of his life and say to myself, "*That's* who Andy was." I was able to recognize what his purpose in this life was, what contributions he made to this world, and what lessons his dying taught us. These were things I was unable to see when he was alive on earth. I was able to recognize him only in the flesh: a typical eighteen-year-old boy with an eighteen-year-old's interests and aggravations. Before his death, I didn't look for any purpose in his life or lessons to be learned from his existence. He was just my son. I took his existence for granted and assumed that he would learn from me, not the other way around. In the death of a loved one our eyes are often opened in unimagined ways and our vision becomes clearer. If we are unable to see purpose in their death, at least we can see purpose in their life.

Father, there are many things I don't understand about this life. I trust in your wisdom to reveal to me what I need to learn at the appropriate time. Send me your spirit to help me

*to continue my thirst for under-
standing and knowledge, and guide
me in that knowledge.*

With the fearful strain that is on me night and
day, if I did not laugh I should die.

—ABRAHAM LINCOLN

Abraham Lincoln knew the meaning of bereavement.
He saw his mother and sons buried. He grieved with
the families of his citizenry who lost their sons on bloody
battlefields. One might wonder where Lincoln could find
it within him to laugh at all. I don't think I have ever seen
a likeness of a smiling Lincoln. He looked like such a sad
man, and with good reason for the sadness. Yet, in the
words quoted above, he speaks of needing laughter as if his
life depended upon it. And it probably did. Our spirits
need laughter for nourishment.

There are times in the early days of bereavement when
you are sure there will never again be laughter in your life
again. I, who had once been able to find humor in even the
most dire circumstance, doubted that I would ever smile
again. As the weeks went by, however, I would find myself
starting to laugh about something and I would catch
myself and wonder, "How can I be laughing again when
Andy is dead?"

Eventually, though, I began to realize that denying
laughter in my life would be a mockery of Andy's memory. Andy was famous for making everyone around him dissolve into laughter. How could he be happy in his new life
if he thought his dying had robbed us of one of his greatest gifts? I also realized that I could laugh when I wanted
to and it wouldn't mean that I loved my son any less or
accepted his death any more. I determined to live my life
as a tribute to my son. If I enjoyed myself, it would be

because I believed myself to be a better person for having had Andy in my life for eighteen years, and that my life had been blessed for having known him.

There are times, even now, years after Andy's death, when I will find myself enjoying a huge laugh and I'll catch myself thinking, "Wow! I'm actually laughing again." Before Andy died, I laughed with no sense of wonder at the act. Yet, after passing through days when I strongly doubted that I would ever experience the tiniest hint of mirth ever again, I realize what a gift the ability to laugh actually is. Laughter is a song of triumph. It is a song of faith and a song of hope. It is our cry to the universe that we are undefeated by the sorrows and hardships of this life. Laughter is a hymn about overcoming obstacles and a prayer of trust that our God will comfort us and bring us joy. Our mourning prayers are prayers of hope in the Savior's promise that our tears of sadness will one day become tears of joy.

I could also laugh and begin to enjoy life again because I knew that Andy continued in his new life where we would someday be with him, and I knew that angels and saints were now enjoying the benefits of his humor. When we believe that God is in our lives, it is possible to be joyful, even in the midst of great sorrow. Try not to cling too tightly to this grief. Be willing to let laughter reenter your life now and then. Become familiar with it again. It is good medicine for the soul, and it does not dishonor the memory of your loved one. Remember the times your loved one brought you laughter, and allow yourself to feel the pleasure of those memories.

Father, let me think back today on all the times my loved one brought laughter into my life. Those were times when I loved him/her the most. Thank you for giving us those good times together. Let me once again enjoy the gift of laughter, and let me share it with those around me. May I bring a smile to someone's face today who might not otherwise have had a reason for joy. God of laughter, be with me this day.

Time of Renewal

Death is nothing at all—I have only slipped away into the next room. I am I and you are you. Whatever we were to each other, that we still are. Call me by my old familiar name, speak to me in the easy way you always used. Wear no forced air of solemnity or sorrow . . . I am waiting for you—for an interval—somewhere near just around the corner. All is well.

—HENRY SCOTT HOLLAND (1847-1918)

The older I get the more I have come to acknowledge the reality of how fleeting this life on earth is. Older relatives who were the mainstays of my childhood have long since left this world. I see my parents, aunts, and uncles growing older and weaker. A few friends have died before it seemed their time. And so very unexpectedly, my own son has died. People who are important members of our communities and lives are here for a while, and then they are gone. I know that eventually we will all follow those who have gone before us into eternity.

I believe that those who have left this world are still very nearby, almost as if, as Holland writes above, they have slipped into the next room, or are just around the corner. Their memories live on within me; I often smile when I recall good times spent with these dear departed ones, and I talk to them regularly. Death has not cut me off from those whose lives are bound to mine. They remain with me in their spiritual embodiment, and I continually send them my love and prayers.

I know that, as spiritual beings, we all pass through this life and on to the next one. We learn how to love while we are here, and we treasure the thoughts and memories of those we have loved and will always love. What a beautiful thing it is to know that we will all be together again someday.

*Father, love connects all souls in heaven
and on earth with you. Keep us united
in your endless love for all eternity.*

Death is just a change in lifestyles.

—STEPHEN LEVINE

This has been a difficult month for my husband's family. Another family friend was buried today. Bill was a wonderfully funny, humorous person. He always had a tease for one of the kids, and they loved to tease back. In turn, his own friends teased him mercilessly for his thrifty ways. We would often see him leaving Mass pointing to his watch and grinning if the priest had used up Bill's allotted time for attending Mass. In his last few years, Bill had suffered greatly from arthritis, and a month before his death, he discovered that he had lung cancer. His body finally betrayed him, as one day all of our own bodies will, and Death claimed this good man.

Yet, as Stephen Levine states, "Death is but a change in lifestyles." I'm sure Bill adjusted to his new lifestyle very quickly: a lifestyle with no pain, no sorrow, and no worry. There is no change in personality when we reach our Home, so I'm sure Bill is as ornery as ever as he settles into his eternal home. His family will mourn his passing for a very long time and will feel his absence. It is my hope that they will also feel his mischievous presence from time to time.

*Risen Lord, welcome all of our loved
ones into your kingdom. As they begin
their wonderful new life in their true
home, let them be overcome with joy
and peacefulness. Let all memories of
past sorrows be wiped away from their*

minds and may they know the won-
ders you have promised. Keep them
also close to us here on earth. Hear
their prayers for us, as you hear our
prayers for them. May we all be unit-
ed in you forever.

Before birth, beings are not manifest to our human senses. In the interim between birth and death, they are manifest. At death they return to the unmanifest again. What is there in all this to grieve over?

—Bhagavad-Gita

Living is death; dying is life. We are not what we appear to be. On this side of the grave we are exiles, on that citizens; on this side orphans, on that children.

—Henry Ward Beecher

When my son departed this earth, I realized for the first time in my life that I truly am an exile here. When a part of my being died along with my child, I understood that our true home is a home far removed from the pain and suffering that we are called to endure on this earth.

I recall the afternoon of my grandniece's birth. She was born a month early and initially had some problems common to premature babies. I thought of little Madolyne's struggle to be born and realized how closely the act of dying resembles being born. Madolyne wasn't prepared to leave the safety and warmth of the only existence she knew, just as we are often not prepared to part with loved ones who die before their time. It is during times such as birth and death that we realize that our timetables are not necessarily what our Father has intended for us. For those of us who have awaited Madolyne's birth, we are overjoyed to see her and welcome her into our world. We surround her with our love and rejoice in her existence. She is totally unaware of all of us. She doesn't know how much we've anticipated her arrival. This world is a strange, noisy, frightening new place for her, and we all want to hold her, kiss her, exult in her, and promise her that she will love it here when she gets a chance to get used to it. We want to reassure her that her new life will be a thousand times more rewarding than her dark, safe environment within her mother's womb. Even as Madolyne grew underneath her mother's heart, she had no knowledge of the being who gave her life, who sustained her life, and who loved her more than her own life. Now she will get to know this person so intimately that she will call out to her in the night, she will run to her when she's frightened or hurt, and she will learn to love her back.

Our transition from this world into the next is not so very different from our birth. We are surrounded now by an all-loving Being who loves us with a passionate tenderness, and who will one day welcome us eagerly into a new life with him, where we will come to know and love him more fully than ever before. And at that time, we will be truly alive, and finally home.

> *Father, you love us deeply even when we don't recognize you or know you. Like a new mother you wait with joyful anticipation for the day we call out your name in love.*

There was never a time when I did not exist, nor you, nor any of these kings. Nor is there any future in which we shall cease to be. Just as the dweller in this body passes through childhood, youth, and old age, so at death he merely passes into another kind of body. The wise are not deceived by that.

—Bhagavad-Gita

I feel Andy's presence around me quite often. When I am especially sad about his death, I feel him drawing closer to me. I've never seen him, or touched him, but a tiny soothing stirring deep within me, a sense of peace, signals his nearness to me. When I am away from home, traveling or on vacation, and my thoughts turn toward him with a sense of melancholy that he is not here to share the experience with me, I feel him near. His handsome young body, his bright smile and piercing blue eyes are gone from me forever, and though I miss them painfully, they are no more to him than a pair of outgrown shoes or an old coat.

When I see pictures of a two-year-old Andy, or a seven-year-old or fourteen-year-old Andy, I acknowledge that the body he inhabited at those ages looked nothing like the eighteen-year-old body from which his spirit finally took leave. Andy's new body in turn looks nothing like his eighteen-year-old self, and I will accustom myself one day to acceptance of his new form. He will always be my son. His spirit is who he is, and I will never be separated from his beautiful soul.

Jesus, you showed us that death would not overcome your people. Even though our physical bodies must one day perish, we rejoice with all the saints and angels in heaven in your triumph over death.

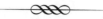

Death is beautiful when seen to be a law and not an accident—It is as common as life.

—HENRY DAVID THOREAU, "ON DEATH"

It's difficult to accept the fact that death is a part of our lives. Death is a natural event. Yet at times, when a person dies suddenly or accidentally, our grief causes us to view this death as unnatural. It seemed completely contradictory to my view of the natural order of life that I should outlive my child. His death was a huge rending of the fabric of the lives of his family and friends. But when I could entertain the idea that from the beginning of time Andy's life on this earth was ordained to last eighteen years, and that his return Home was a part of the progression of his soul's life, the concept of death lost some of its horror. Death is no more and no less than the next step we take in our spiritual journey.

We each enter this life as infants, and we each age progressively until death takes us into the next stage of our development. It is not something to be feared. As a people of faith, we do not see death as an ending, but rather, as a beginning.

Lord, I accept the gift you have given me in my grief to be able to understand that death is no longer an enemy. You have promised eternal life to all your children. May all of my loved ones who rest in your arms today

delight in the joys that you have prom-
ised us.

Death is nothing but a change of form.
Material dies to become a robe. Wood dies to
become furniture. Clay dies to become brick.
Brick dies to become wall and building. Death
is just transformation from one form to another form. The previous form is dead; the new
form is born.

—WILLIAM ELLIOTT, *TYING ROCKS TO CLOUDS: MEETINGS*
AND CONVERSATIONS WITH WISE AND SPIRITUAL PEOPLE,
INTERVIEW WITH SWAMI SATCHIDANANDA

My mother used to laughingly tell the story of the time
she took my younger sister Jill to the doctor for a
check-up. When the doctor asked Jill what she wanted to be
when she grew up, Jill replied with all the seriousness of a
three-year-old, "A bird." Perhaps in the subconscious of
each of us there is a longing to rise and soar above the earth,
to fly. Our mortal bodies are not equipped for such a feat,
but the longing is there nevertheless. Is it possible that this
yearning originates in our souls, the part of us that is truly
able to soar when it is not earthbound by the body it inhabits? How glorious the release of death must be for the spirit, when it is freed from the bonds of this earth and allowed
to soar and rise toward the Creator. This, I believe, is what
we were created for, and our spirits long for that day.

Father, let me always remember that I
am a spiritual being. I am so much
more than the body I inhabit, a body
that ages each day and will die. I am
an eternal being who will one day be

*reunited with all those who have gone
before me. Let me keep my eyes always
on the horizon of eternity.*

I consider that what we suffer at this present
time cannot be compared at all with the glory
that is going to be revealed to us.

—ROMANS 8:18

"The mountains and hills may crumble, but
my love for you will never end; I will keep forever my promise of peace." So says the Lord
who loves you.

—ISAIAH 54:10

From the earliest moments after the birth of Christianity,
the fathers of the new religion were emphatic in their
assurances to the new and sometimes bewildered flock of
believers that this world was a world of trial into which we
were born. But they were quick to promise that an eternal
life of great and unbelievable happiness awaited us in the
next world after our death. These early Christians must
have had a very powerful and sustaining faith in this promise. One after another, the leaders of this new religion,
beginning with Jesus himself, were publicly and horribly
put to death. Yet rather than scattering this timid little
flock, they were strengthened and empowered by each
martyr's death.

When I stood in St. Peter's Basilica in the Vatican several months ago and listened to the guide narrate the story
of the discovery of Peter's tomb, I saw those early martyrs
as real people who had once lived and walked on the very
spot where I now stood two thousand years later. I was
strengthened by the faith of those early Christians who had

traveled to Peter's tomb in the months and years after his death and etched the words "Ask Peter" on the walls. These words were a stunning affirmation of their belief in Peter's continuing existence into eternity. These same people had seen Peter die a most horrible death, a death designed to test the faith of the strongest believer. Yet they encouraged each other to "ask Peter" to pray for them. Death had no power over these early Christians. They were convinced beyond any possible doubt that the promises of eternal life were true. Their convictions were strong enough to be passed down from generation to generation through two millennia until this present time. They give us courage even today.

Jesus, your promise of eternal life has sustained us for thousands of years. Your message is still heard by those who believe in you. Never let us forget these promises.

I tell my patients, "Death alters relationships; it does not sever them. The physical body is gone but the personal relationship lives on inside you."

—EDIE DEVERS, *GOODBYE AGAIN*

It was such an enormous relief to me to understand that my relationship with my son was not severed by his physical death. I could indeed still have a relationship with him. It's not the relationship I would have preferred if I'd been given a choice. Naturally, I'd much rather see him clomp in the back door grinning at me, making muddy trails into the kitchen. But, accepting the impossibility of this, it is wonderful to know that, in spirit, he is still coming through that back door, smiling at me, living forever in my memories of him. I have days that I am happy for my son, happy for his freedom from these earthly bonds, for the glory of his new life. I am comforted to know that he is still as close to me as my next breath, that he celebrates with his family and rejoices in our little joys. I feel calmed to know that he watches over his family and his friends, that he lives both with us and with God.

It doesn't take all the pain of his death away. I miss him every day. My first waking thoughts in the morning and my last conscious thoughts in the evening are of Andy. I still weep for the loss of him, but I know that our relationship is not over. It's just a matter of getting used to our new relationship, the one that will never end.

Lord, you promised to be with us until the end of time. Walk with us today. Help us to remember your promise of everlasting life and strengthen our faith in your words. As our loved ones now live in your light and love, let us always try to draw closer to that light by our actions here in this life.

Death is not the end, it is simply walking out of the physical form and into the spirit realm, which is our true home. It's going back home.

—STEPHEN CHRISTOPHER, QUOTED IN *HELLO FROM HEAVEN!*, BY BILL AND JUDY GUGGENHEIM

How comforting it is to think of heaven as home. Andy is not in some strange, frightening land, or even in a new and wonderful place. He is simply home. He is in a place that is comfortable and familiar, a place where he knows he belongs and can be at peace and safe.

Shortly after Andy's death, as I wrote about earlier, Jill had a dream in which she saw written in the sky a message from Andy, "Hi, Mom, I'm home." When I heard those words from my daughter, I felt an enormous burden lifting from my broken heart. My son was not lost, or wandering, or even far away. He was home. Home is the place we yearn for, an end of a journey, a haven, a place of acceptance and love and welcome.

From that moment on, I no longer worried about Andy's whereabouts or his welfare. I continued with my grieving because I will always miss his physical presence, but I will never again worry about him. He is safe. He's home.

Father, your angels rejoice when one of your children reaches the shores of their eternal home. We who are left behind look forward with faith to the day that our own journey is over and we will be reunited with those who have gone before us and who live with and in you forever. Keep our eyes always on the road that leads us safely Home.

———— ∞ ————

"Death shall be the last enemy," said Jesus. What He meant was that we should no longer perceive death as an enemy. We would recognize that death is not death but recycling of energy, a remodulation of the cells according to higher assignments in a soul's progression.

> The spirit does not die, but rather enters new channels of life.
>
> —MARIANNE WILLIAMSON, *ILLUMINATA*

I wonder what life after death is like. Many have speculated. Some have claimed authoritatively to know exactly what the afterlife is like. Others have denied that there is an afterlife. We each have our own idea of what we would hope our life after death is, but none of us can claim to know exactly what awaits us until we ourselves walk through those portals.

If we read the words of Jesus, we can get a glimmer of an idea of what's in store for us. Jesus promises us that every tear will be wiped away, so it's perhaps safe to assume that heaven will be a place free of sorrow or pain. He promises us that his Father's house has many mansions. Thus perhaps we can assume that heaven will be different things to different people. Jesus assured his followers that he was going to prepare a place for them, so we can believe that he is making sure that heaven is exactly the state of being that we each hope it will be.

I imagine that heaven is a real place, and that we will have real bodies, and everything around and about us will be filled with indescribable beauty and peace. I believe that I will once again see my loved ones who have gone before me, and that the light of God's love will completely envelop us. Knowing what awaits me, believing in this, allows me to embrace this present life with a joyful spirit, a spirit that rejoices in the beauty of this life and anticipates the glory of the next life.

> *God, giver of hope, you encourage me with your promise of eternal life. I thank you for the gift of all life, of all living things in this universe, and of all life still to be experienced.*

I cannot understand why anyone should fear death. . . . I believe that when the eyes without my physical eyes shall open upon the world to come, I shall simply be consciously living in the country of my heart.

—HELEN KELLER

How wonderful to think of our afterlife as Helen Keller did, as the country of our hearts. I wonder if Helen Keller, deprived as she was of two of life's most important senses, vision and hearing, was able to develop her inner vision more fully than the rest of us. I wonder if she was more attuned to the country of her heart than I am. Without the distractions offered by the gifts of seeing and hearing with her physical eyes and ears, perhaps she was free to travel more closely to that place where her human body wasn't necessary to behold the wonders of creation. In her writings she seems to have a keen sense of the eternity of life, and she knew no fear of the darkness we call death.

If we could become familiar with the countries of our own hearts, then perhaps our spiritual eyes and ears will be opened to mysteries unfolding all around us in this universe. And when the time comes for us to lay aside these earthly bodies, we will not be traveling to a strange or frightening country. We will simply be returning home. In order to do this, we need to close our physical eyes and ears for a while each day, and get in touch with our souls. In this silence when we allow the eyes and ears of our souls to observe this world, we will hear the whispering of the God who lives in each of us.

Divine Creator, in the silence of my soul I listen for your voice. Open my ears, my eyes, and my mind, that when I am in your presence I will

*know you, I will experience your peace
and love, and I will be comforted by
the wonders of your existence. Increase
my awareness of your dwelling within
me, and let me always remember that
you are near.*

Each night is but the past day's funeral, and the
morning his resurrection: why then should our
funeral sleep be otherwise than our sleep at
night?

—ARTHUR WARWICK, *SPARE MINUTES*, 1637

When my mother tucked me in at night when I was
very young, we prayed this prayer: "Now I lay me
down to sleep, I pray the Lord my soul to keep. If I
should die before I wake, I pray the Lord my soul to
take." I had no idea then what a soul was. As I mentioned
earlier, I had a picture in my child's mind of a soul looking something like one of the California Raisins. Whatever
they were, I figured, if I were to die, the Lord was more
than welcome to keep that little creature. But I don't
remember giving more than a passing amount of concern
to the thought that I might not awaken after the night's
sleep. I went to my dreams confident of rising with the
dawn each morning. We should have the same attitude
about the sleep of our eventual death. We should meet
death with the confidence of our awakening in the morning to an eternal dawn.

*Lord, be near me each night as I lay
my body down to rest. Be near me in
the morning as I begin my day. Be
beside me when the evening of my life*

*comes, and gently awaken me into
your eternal home.*

I never think of a friend after his death as now
resting in a sleep of peace. I cannot believe that
he has passed to the state of personal inactivity
which the words suggest. I am more completely sure that he has passed to more life and more
activity, to a state of greatly increased spiritual
awareness and exercise.

—Archbishop Fisher (former Archbishop of
Canterbury), *Church Times,* 9/23/66

My mother had a dream not long after Andy died. In
her dream she was at her grandmother's house.
Mamo, as we called her, was preparing a large family dinner. When we were growing up, Mamo would extend the
seating at her dining room table by placing a long board
between two chairs. In her dream, my mother was watching Mamo prepare the meal when the phone rang. My
great-grandmother told Mom to get the phone, saying,
"It's probably Andy, calling to say he'll be late." My mother
answered the phone and it was indeed Andy, saying, "Hey,
I'll be there for dinner but I'm running late. And I'm
NOT sitting on that board for dinner." It sounded so like
Andy that I laughed when my mother recounted the
dream to me.

But the idea of my great-grandmother, whom I dear-
ly loved, preparing Sunday dinner for the great-great-
grandson she had never met on this earth, filled me with
a warm feeling. It is entirely possible that my loved ones
are together in heaven, enjoying things they enjoyed on
earth. It is a curiously peaceful idea for me to think that
family is caring for Andy even now. I'm not sure what

heaven will be like, but if it involves Sunday dinner at Mamo's with all of my loved ones, I can hardly wait to get there. I'll even sit on the board.

> *Lord, in your Father's house of many mansions, there is a place where my own family dwells now. If my prayers for them can make their mansion more comfortable, please hurry these prayers home to them. Tell them to keep the light on for me in expectation of the happy day of my own homecoming.*

"Never again will they hunger or thirst; neither sun nor any scorching heat will burn them, because the Lamb, who is in the center of the throne, will be their shepherd, and he will guide them to springs of life-giving water. And God will wipe away every tear from their eyes."

—REVELATION 7:16-17

The power of God is greater than death. Our relationships are not severed at death, but refocused beyond physical connection. As our vision of life changes, so will the physical world. As we lift our eyes above the illusion of death, we will begin to see the eternity of life.

—MARIANNE WILLIAMSON, *ILLUMINATA*

When we learned of Andy's death in the early morning hours of his father's birthday, "death" was a concept that was simply too huge, too immense and overwhelming for us to grasp. It is said that there is certain finality to death, but if this is so, that finality didn't register with us until much later. The idea of a child's death was so horrifying that we weren't able to assimilate the fact of it for many months. Awareness washed over us in waves each waking hour. It took me many weeks to understand what "death" meant: he wouldn't be walking in the door, we wouldn't hear his voice, we wouldn't celebrate holidays with him, his things would have to be put away, he wouldn't call on the phone. All of these realizations and many more settled in on us gradually, and each settling brought new pain.

As I write this page, it is the anniversary of the day Andy died on his father's forty-seventh birthday. It is a day of immeasurable sadness when we remember the horror of those hours when the unthinkable idea of his death became a reality. I look back on that day in 1997, and I know that there will never again in my life be a sadness to equal the grief of that day. It was a morning when I felt that God had removed himself from our presence, and any angels who may have been hovering over our little family had slipped away with Andy's departure. I was completely emptied of any spark of hope or joy in those hours and believed that the flames of my passions would never heat again. I remembered how Jesus cried in his despair, "My God, why have you forsaken me?" and I knew for the first time the loneliness of the cross.

And then came the gift: the knowing of God's presence, feeling his quiet strength which death could not subdue, and the changing of our vision. The realization that, as Marianne Williamson writes, our relationships are not severed, but refocused, is a great gift, a gift that gives us comfort and hope. It is a gift that permits us to open our eyes and look beyond the physical world into eternity. And when we look into that eternity, we finally know peace.

The anniversary of Andy's death will always be a sad day for us. But on the other hand, what a wonderful day it was for my son, who had been led into his Father's arms, led back to his real and only home. How he must have rejoiced to be home again! At first it seemed such a cruel twist of fate that Andy should have left this life on his father's birthday. But now we understand that Pat and Andy share a birthdate: Andy was born into his eternal life on the day his father was born into his earthly life. Perhaps it was meant to honor his father in a way we at first couldn't understand in the midst of our grief.

> *Lord, I lean into your power, and put my trust in your love. You will hold me closely through this day and night. My song of mourning will be yours also, and your song of joy will become mine as I reach for eternity.*

The meaning of death is not the annihilation of the spirit, but its separation from the body, and that the resurrection and day of assembly do not mean a return to a new existence after annihilation, but the bestowal of a new form or frame to the spirit.

—AL-GHAZZALI, *ALCHEMY OF HAPPINESS*

I think about Andy each day, but I now spend less time mourning the loss of his future on this earth for I know that he lives within and around me. He is closer than my next thought. When I think of his life on this earth, the memories more often than not bring a smile to my face. I've come to accept the idea that his beautiful human form was only a reflection of his glorious eternal self. His body was no more than a temporary dwelling—a dwelling that each of us treasures for now, but which we will each shed with gladness when it is our time to soar into eternal life.

I am naturally very attached to my physical body, even with all of its flaws and imperfections, its annoying aches and pains. I am relatively young and my body has not betrayed me yet with the hardships of old age or ill health. I would like to continue to inhabit this home of my soul as long as possible because I know that in the perspective of eternity, I shall only be here for a heartbeat. I'd like to enjoy all that I can during this wonderful interlude. But I know that this home was not designed for permanence. I am merely a tenant on this earth, not an owner. Soon I will pass from this place just as the millions of souls who have gone before me. Whereas in the past, I dreaded the idea of the end—of death—I now look forward to a day of wonderful reunions.

> *Eternal God, may we always remember that it is in you that we have our being, a being that was designed for existence in your home in heaven for all time. I give you thanks for the days of this life that you have given me, and I look forward with hope to the day of my homecoming.*

I felt that any new definition [of death] had to go beyond the death of the physical body. I had to consider the proof we had that man also had a soul and spirit, a higher reason for life, a poetry, something more than mere existence and survival, something that continued on.

—Elisabeth Kübler-Ross, *The Wheel of Life*

> We are not human beings having a spiritual
> experience. We are spiritual beings having a
> human experience.
>
> —PIERRE TEILHARD DE CHARDIN

The above quote moved me profoundly when I read it shortly after Andy's death. It gave a greater degree of meaning to this existence. It helped me to understand that our life on this planet is brief and fleeting, and we are merely visitors here. Our true home, the home we unconsciously long for all of our days, lies within eternity. It gave me a warm feeling to realize that my precious child, like all of the rest of us, was merely passing through this life, and was returning to his true home, the home to which his spirit had strained since his birth. I knew that we all are in a state of yearning toward home, yet some of us must live in this exile longer than others. I realized then that Andy would never be homesick for this existence where his presence was so sorely missed. Andy would never know homesickness again. His spirit was home. With his enlightened understanding of eternity, he would know that our separation would only be a moment and our reunion would be everlasting. When I read this quote for the first time, I felt the early stirrings of my own spirit's awakening. I began to recognize that self who was not at home on this earth and who longed always for Home. This is the part of my self that walks with God.

When I realize that I truly am an eternal being, I am able to embrace this life much more fully than ever before. I have a knowledge that whatever suffering I am called to endure in this life is only momentary when viewed through eternal eyes. The sorrows and fears of this life lose some of their power over me when I remember that they cannot ultimately destroy me. When I cast aside my fear of death, I can then reach out to this life and allow myself to savor every experience and to treasure each moment of this life.

When I mourn those who have died and gone home, I am comforted knowing that my grieving is only a temporary state, that one day we will all be reunited again and there will be no more grief.

My prayer this day is a prayer of love. It is a prayer of longing for our loved ones and our belief in a day of reunion. It is an acknowledgment of the fact that if we had not loved we would not mourn, and therefore our very mourning is a celebration of great love.

Holy Spirit, we long for our eternal home. Our spirits are restless in this exile. Keep us close to you, so that we might be reminded of our true beginnings. Enlighten our minds that we might come to know our spiritual selves more intimately, and open our hearts that we might let your love pour into us.

The more we dwell on the happy state of our departed, the closer we shall be to them.

—HELEN KELLER

I have to believe that sorrow and grief are inescapable conditions of humanity. It's what we learn from these hardships and how we grow through adversity that finally determines what we will accomplish in this lifetime. If we lock ourselves away and dwell on our pain to the exclusion of everything else, we cannot grow. Sometimes it's very difficult to tear ourselves away from our mourning when someone very close to us has died. We grieve for them, we miss them, and we physically hurt from the pain of the loss.

But if we can turn our thoughts to the "happy state" of our loved ones, as Helen Keller calls it, we cannot possibly let the grief consume us. We can lay aside for a while our own sense of loss and rejoice for our loved ones who are now beyond all earthly sorrows and pains.

I find myself wishing happiness on my son and praying for his well-being now that he is out of my earthly care. It's the only way I can still "mother" him. When I pray for Andy, I ask Jesus and his Mother to hold him for me, to let him feel the love of all those he has left behind, and to let him know that in spite of our sorrow, we rejoice for him in his new life and celebrate his joy. In doing so, I can feel my own spirits lift. I feel closer to heaven myself, and then, as Helen Keller promises, I feel Andy draw closer to me. I can begin to share a little of his own peace.

> *Lord, bless and keep our loved ones who have died. Let them share in the joy of your eternal life. You have promised us each a home where all tears shall be wiped away. We believe that our loved ones now share in your promises, and we live in hope for the day that all of us will be together with you forever.*

My mother and sister must be very happy to be home with God and I am sure their love and prayers are always with me. When I go home to God, for death is nothing else but going home to God, the bond of love will be unbroken for all eternity.

—MOTHER TERESA

As I sit writing this, my children are scattered. Sean is probably packing his things in preparation for a move to a new house he has bought. Jill is in Seattle finishing her college classes, and Julie is out fishing with friends. I think about each of them often during the day, and I still take their problems to heart and worry about them when they are troubled. I think of Andy each day also, but I no longer worry about him. I know that he is safe, he is happy and no harm will ever again befall him.

I'll see Julie in a few hours when she returns home. I'll probably see Sean this weekend when we help him move. I'll see Jill in a week when I fly out to Seattle to accompany her on the drive home. I'll see Andy again one day also. I'm not sure of the exact day or time, but it is a date that I hold dear to my heart. Someday we will all have wonderful reunions.

> *God of homecomings, my mourning song today is a song of hope. It is a song of belief in the future and anticipation of the joyous reunions we will experience on the day of our Homecoming. Let me appreciate every day the precious gift of life that you have given me, and let me glorify you with my use of this gift until the day you bring me back to you.*

We cannot describe the natural history of the soul, but we know that it is divine.

—RALPH WALDO EMERSON, *THE METHOD OF NATURE*, 1849

What a consolation to be able to believe in the divinity of the soul. How fortunate we are to know that our loved ones continue on, that they still exist, and that their love is still with us. It makes the memories of their lives here with us all the sweeter. When we think of them, we aren't overcome with a sense of futility. We realize that all of us are spiritual beings who are having a temporary human experience. My heart aches for those who are not blessed with this belief. How much more painfully their loss must feel, thinking that the separation is forever.

Although I miss my son terribly and would give all I had in the world to be able to hold him again, I am strengthened by the certainty that this separation is no more permanent than if he had moved to a distant land. I know that I will be with him again. At times he is still very close to me. I feel his love and know that he aches for the happiness of those who miss him. For his sake, we will live every day to the fullest.

Lord, all of us share in your divine life. Keep those who have left this world close to you. Give them joy and peace in their new lives. Let your love overwhelm them and fill them with wonder and awe. Keep all of us close to you until we are reunited once again for all time.

According to Yorick Spiegel, it is a long-term feature of bereavement that the dead person is not abandoned or forgotten. "But the form of his presence has changed; it no longer is bound to his personal appearance, which dissolves in the memory, just as does his body. He becomes a possession, never to be lost, by being restored within the bereaved."

—NICHOLAS PETER HARVEY, *DEATH'S GIFT: CHAPTERS ON RESURRECTION AND BEREAVEMENT*

O ur loved ones never truly die. They merely change form and we, in time, learn to establish a new and deeper relationship with those who have gone before us. As the years pass, the memory of the sound of a loved one's voice becomes a little fuzzy. It becomes harder and harder to recall the physical features of the loved one without the aid of photographs, but this in no way signifies that we are forgetting the loved one. As the Bible states, could a mother ever forget her baby?

Our relationships with those who have departed do not end. They grow and develop in new ways. We eventually come to understand that our loved ones do indeed live on within us in a manner that is much more than just symbolic. We feel their presence around us, we share love, we look to them for guidance and comfort, and we both await the day of reunion. Our relationships with our loved ones, we eventually realize, will continue to grow and change for all eternity. When we understand this we are comforted to know that love is indeed eternal.

Lord, make me aware of your ever-present Spirit. Remind me that we, like you, are eternal beings whose true home is in heaven with you. Remind us when we weep for the loss of those we love that our separation is neither permanent nor complete. We all live in you now and forever.

> The resurrection of Jesus is seen as decisive for all bereavement. . . . "Do not cling to Me" is of the essence, meaning, "If you cling to me as I was, then I cannot be with you now as I am."
>
> —NICHOLAS PETER HARVEY, *DEATH'S GIFT: CHAPTERS ON RESURRECTION AND BEREAVEMENT*

I had such trouble letting go of Andy in his death. I kept seeing his smiling, eighteen-year-old face, and listening for his voice in my mind. I waited for him to come in the door, I searched for him in crowds of young people, and I picked up the phone expecting to hear his voice. My brain rebelled at the idea that these experiences were over forever, that I would never see my son again in this life. That horrible knowledge took quite some time to sink in.

Now, with the passage of time, I understand that my relationship with Andy is not over. It has merely changed, just as it has always changed and grown during our lives together. Our relationship when he was in diapers was not the same as the relationship we had when he started playing football, but we were still connected as mother and son. Our relationship today is different also. Our connection is now spiritual instead of physical, but our bond as mother and child remains unbroken, and will endure forever.

In time I'll get used to our new relationship, just as I needed time to adjust to his passage from childhood to adolescence. But the love between us will only grow stronger with the passage of each day, and I will grow more joyful, knowing that I haven't lost my son after all.

Jesus, in your resurrection you showed us for all time that life continues beyond the grave. You have given us this hope to sustain us in our despair and comfort us in our sorrow. Keep

this promise before us in our darkest
times to give us courage.

When we learn how to say good-bye we truly learn how to say to ourselves and others: "Go, God be with you. I entrust you to God. The God of strength, courage, comfort, hope, love is with you. The God who promises to wipe away all tears will hold you close and will fill your emptiness. Let go and be free to move on. Do not keep yourself from another step in your homeward journey. May the blessing of the God of Autumn be with you."

—JOYCE RUPP, *PRAYING OUR GOODBYES*

There comes a difficult time in our grief journey when we are ready to acknowledge to ourselves that this separation is a reality, and it is time to wish our loved ones Godspeed on their journeys into eternity. This was a difficult moment for me. Although intellectually I knew that Andy was dead and that I would not see him again in this life, accepting and acknowledging that idea were more difficult than I had imagined. Yet there did come a time, one morning as I sat reading Joyce Rupp's Praying Our Goodbyes, that I was able to say to my son, "Go with God, Andy. I release you into the hands of your eternal Father. Be happy and keep my love with you." This was not for quite some time after Andy had died. I imagined a great weight being lifted from my son's shoulders as he accepted my release. This was a fearsome thing for me to do because I feared that in saying goodbye I would sever my ties with my son as he moved away from me.

That has not been the case though. Andy will always be as close as my next breath. This was another lesson I learned about our existence in eternity. Time and space do not separate us from those we love. Saying goodbye was not, after all, for Andy's benefit, but for my own. In releasing Andy I was merely saying to myself, "I understand that I will not see you again on this earth. I accept our new relationship." So, in the end, saying goodbye was actually saying hello: goodbye to our old way of relating and hello to a new existence.

> *Lord, when you left this earth you told your followers that the separation was only for a while and then they would see you again. We look forward in faith until the day when we see you for all eternity and we have faith that our loved ones already share in your promise.*

Death is but our visible horizon, and our look ought always to be focused beyond it. We should never talk as if death were the end of anything.

—GEORGE MACDONALD

One of my final memories of Andy was at the last Fourth of July party of his life. We had had a cookout at our house and our backyard was filled with family and friends. I remember sitting on the patio visiting with our guests as the night grew old. Toward the end of the evening, Andy and his friend Jennie came back and sat down. Jill walked over and sat on Andy's knee and proceeded to tell everyone around us what a great brother Andy was. She bragged that she and Andy had never had a fight in their lives. I remember the warm feeling I had watching my beautiful children laughing and joking, and loving each other. It was one of those perfect evenings when all seems right with the world and life looks wonderful. Three weeks later he was dead.

I treasure the memory of that night. A year later on the following Fourth of July, I was lying in the pool trying not to let memories of the previous summer cause too much pain. As I was floating in the water I happened to look up and saw that my nephew Tim, and Brad, one of Andy's oldest and dearest friends, had stopped by. I closed my eyes as a wall of pain flooded over me, and I wished that Andy could be here with his friends on this day. As I opened my eyes I noticed the look on Brad's face, and I knew that he and I were sharing the same thought. At that moment, a feeling of deep peace came over me and I knew that our wish had come true. Andy was indeed with us, and would always be with us, whenever we thought of him or needed him. Death is not the end of love.

Father, I hope always in the promises of your kingdom. I entrust my loved ones into your divine care, in the belief that they now share in your eternal joy. Keep them at your side and may they be filled with happiness for all eternity.

God's miracle moments are reminders that He is orchestrating a grand plan for our eternal benefit. All things, large and small, are being fitted together for the greater good that He has created for us. As you grieve, don't miss the miracle moments that God will surely send your way. Recognize His hand at work. Accept His gifts of joy to you as you see, not coincidences, but blessings and miracles.

—ZIG ZIGLAR, *CONFESSIONS OF A GRIEVING CHRISTIAN*

> I think death is a tremendous adventure—a gateway into a new life, in which you have further powers, deeper joys, and wonderful horizons.
>
> —DR. LESLIE D. WEATHERHEAD, QUOTED IN *LIFE BEGINS AT DEATH*, 1969

> When I pray, coincidences happen, and when I do not, they don't.
>
> —WILLIAM TEMPLE, LATE ARCHBISHOP OF CANTERBURY

Like many bereaved people, I sometimes need a sign from my son that he is okay, that he is still with me. Usually—almost always, in fact—when I pray for such a sign I am given one. A skeptic might well write off these happenings as coincidence, but I have no quarrel with coincidence. I once read a quote that said that coincidences are God's way of remaining anonymous.

In the past few years I have become acutely aware of coincidences all around me. These synchronistic events always have the effect of cheering me up or comforting me when I most need it. Sometimes one of us will find a penny minted in 1979, the year of Andy's birth, at just the time when we are worried or lonely, or in need of cheering up. Other times we'll see the number 66, Andy's football number, or hear one of his favorite songs when we are in trouble or feeling sad.

My in-laws have a collection of pennies that have been found in situations that cause them to believe that they are signs from their grandson reminding them that he still watches over them. Often when they are traveling, they will find a penny in their hotel room or in a restaurant with the dates of either Andy's death or birth years—1997 or 1979.

When my mother and I checked into our hotel room while vacationing in Barcelona, Spain, I happened to glance down on the floor to see a penny lying at my feet. Neither of us had brought any American change. I stooped to retrieve the penny and out of habit looked to check the date. I was not too surprised to see that the date on the penny was 1979, for I knew before I picked the coin up that this was a greeting from my son, a reminder that he is always with us, no matter how far from home we are.

The other day I asked Andy to send me a sign of some sort that he was still nearby. I hadn't felt his presence for some time, and I was missing him. The idea then came to my mind that I would find a dime in an unusual place, and that would be my sign from Andy. The next day as I was standing in the checkout lane in the grocery store, I felt something hit my foot. As I looked down, I saw a dime lying on my shoe. I'm sure that if anyone had been watching me they would have mistaken me for the village idiot by the way I reacted to that dime. Grinning like a fool, I bent down, picked up the coin, and stared at it, turning it over in my hand as if it were a rare gem. There was my sign. But then I looked up and saw a young mother with several children beside her. She was reaching toward me with a hand full of change. "I dropped my dime," she said. Coincidence? Of course. But as far as I can remember, I have never in my life had a dime drop on my foot, and never, I am positive, after asking to find a dime in an unusual spot.

These little coincidences became very commonplace in the early months after Andy's death. I believe that these incidents are tiny gifts from the Creator, gifts given to give us a lift or to remind us that there are powers in our universe that are beyond our understanding or control. When I experience one of these coincidences, it sends a warm feeling of peace through me and I remember again that I am not alone. They have taught me that God seldom displays himself directly to us. Instead he uses the forces of nature, or the actions of other people to show his presence among us. When I experience a meaningful coincidence, I feel God's touch in my life.

Our loved ones do not abandon us in death. They are always beside us, always carrying our needs in their hearts. The little signs that we are able to pick up on are reminders from them to us that love is eternal.

Jesus, you showed your apostles many signs and wonderful visions before and after your death to comfort and reassure them, to convince them of your love and your presence. You allow our loved ones in heaven to send us small reminders of the fact that life is unending and that love's bonds are forever. God, Creator of all things, open my eyes to the mysteries and wonders with which you have surrounded me. Let me become more aware of your presence in each moment of my life.

The longer I live, the more convinced I become that surviving changes us. After the bitterness, the anger, the guilt, and the despair are tempered by time, we look at life differently.

—Erma Bombeck

As long as we live on this earth, we can be considered to be survivors. Some of us survive trauma even though badly injured either physically or spiritually. Some of us walk away from tragedy with barely a scratch on either body or soul. Survival is immediate. If we are still alive we have survived.

Healing takes much longer. As time passes, however, and our wounds begin to heal and become distant memories, we sometimes can be compared to those who have been victims of serious burns. All of the outer layers of our lives are affected. The process of healing involves extreme pain, and when the healing is complete, we may find that we are no longer the same person that we once were. Sometimes the scars disfigure us in one way or another.

Other times the scarring is barely noticeable, but the pain is never far from the surface for many days to come.

Either way, the injury will affect us for the rest of our lives. If we are fortunate, the scars will soften around our souls, open our eyes to the beauty of God's love, and become instruments of healing in themselves. If we are not as fortunate, we will find ourselves shut away from the world by the disfigurement of our scarring and pain. We will shut out the light and turn inward, with sorrow as our only companion. However, unlike a burn victim, we are able to choose the route our healing will take. If we learn to accept God's plan for us and trust in his love, we can expect a beautiful healing.

> *Father, I give my scarred and bat-*
> *tered soul over to your healing hands.*
> *Wash away any anger, bitterness,*
> *guilt, or despair, and make me whole*
> *again.*

Certainly one's relationship with God can be a comfort, a tremendous coping resource throughout every stage of grieving. But as a pathway to transcendence, something different occurs. . . . One's spiritual relationship is nourished, changed, strengthened, enriched *as a result of your loss.* In other words, the experience of loss deepens your relationship with the Divine in a way which didn't exist before and that might not ever have existed were it not for this experience.

—ASHLEY DAVIS PREND, *TRANSCENDING LOSS*

The above paragraph moved me deeply the first time I read it almost two years after Andy's death. In fact, I had been discovering these things for myself, but I was under the impression that these discoveries were something unique to my own grief. I remember talking to my friend Jeff, a priest, a few months after Andy died and telling him that my time of sorrow was a time in which I'd received many gifts. I was at a loss for the words to describe these new sensations, but it was exactly as Prend writes: "a deepening of a relationship with the Divine." I understand now that if I hadn't suffered this great loss, I might never have entered into this precious relationship with my Creator. And I am thankful that out of my life's greatest tragedy emerged a gift of immeasurable value, an awareness of the nearness of God's presence, the depth of his undying love, and the wondrous promise of eternity.

> *Father, in my darkest hour you showed yourself to me. You made me aware of your presence, a presence that not only loved me but also suffered with me. In my time of mourning you never left my side. You comforted and encouraged me. You opened my eyes and displayed before me the beauties of your universe, sights that I had once taken for granted. You saved me from despair with your reminder of eternal life, and you drew me close to your heart. You are my God and my Savior.*

Opening up to the pain of death, our own or that of someone we love, is one of the most mysterious blessings of life. Nothing focuses us more clearly on what matters, helps us drop our defenses more quickly or gives us more compassion for human suffering.

—Marianne Williamson, *Illuminata*

When I was newly bereaved, nothing in the world mattered to me but the pain I was enduring. All the minor annoyances I used to make into major issues became insignificant. Worries about the future became meaningless. The present, as it existed, was overwhelming enough. The earth itself became an ugly, squalid place where despair ruled.

Over time, as the sharp edge of grief began to dull, I noticed that people who had once irritated me began to seem more tolerable. Pet peeves like dirty dishes in the sink or wet towels on the floor did not merit the expenditure of energy it would take to raise a complaint. I found myself softening in my grief, becoming less critical and impatient. I started to develop a sense of acceptance of things beyond my control. And gradually, in very short bursts and then in longer and longer periods, I began to become aware once more of the beauty of our universe. The works of God—mountains, trees, clouds, and oceans—became breathtaking works of divine art, and the arts of humankind—poetry, paintings, and sculpture—became reflections of that divinity. Little by little I was made aware of the powerful beauty of creation, and I basked in the warmth of that realization. I was blessed to be able to hear the sounds of another human brother or sister calling out in their desperation for someone to give them respite. I say I was blessed because in being able to hear their cries, I was able to hear the voice of God calling to me, asking me to participate in his divinity. I have been blessed in my pain.

Father, let me be sensitive to the pain of others around me. Give me the strength and spirit of selflessness needed to reach out to others who are hurting. When I try to ease the discomfort of others, I am also helping myself, and doing the work that you have asked of each one of us.

Many of us spend our whole lives running from feeling with the mistaken belief that you cannot bear the pain. But you have already borne the pain. What you have not done is feel all you are beyond that pain.

—KAHLIL GIBRAN

What an awesome thing it is to be confronted with your greatest nightmare, to live through that experience and survive it, and then to come out on the other side of that fire. Those of us who have endured such a fate are often surprised to look back and realize that we did indeed survive the confrontation. We are sometimes even more surprised to understand that the fire of our suffering has tempered us and made us stronger people than we were before our trial.

When I remember the past, I look back with longing on the days when my family was intact, the nights when my children were safely tucked in bed and no nightmares lurked in our dark hallways. But I don't miss the person that I was before that time of loss. Although I am now a person who carries a deep sadness within the depths of her soul, a sadness I could have done without if asked, I am also a person with a new strength, a stronger faith, and a renewed sense of respect and awe for the world around me.

I have a new thirst for knowledge, a confidence born of adversity, and a great hope for the future.

We can choose to take the sorrows that come our way in this life and allow them to make better people of us. And in so doing, we please our Creator.

> *Jesus, our brother in suffering, you showed the way to eternal life, and you warned us that the path would not be an easy one. When we stumble and fall with the weight of our daily burdens, be with us; help us to remember that we do not carry these burdens alone.*

"Where there is sorrow there is holy ground," Wilde teaches. It is in the healing process that we come to a new appreciation of life. What the human being survives is the mark of the mettle of humanity. What we manage to transcend is what we have triumphed over. What we have wrestled with and won is what measures in us the quality of our lives.

—Joan Chittister, *There Is a Season*

Overcoming grief, transcending it, is a choice that we make each day when we are mourning the loss of a loved one. We can choose to be victims of our grief. We can do as Queen Victoria did upon Albert's death and dress in mourning clothes for the rest of our lives. We can deny ourselves the gifts that are meant to be ours on this earth. We can choose to be locked up in our sadness until our final day. Then again, we can and should choose to enter as fully as possible into this painful sorrow, acknowledge and befriend it, overcome our distaste for it, and begin the process of transcending it. It may take many months or years until we are able to look up and see the sunlight of happiness again, but we should be confident that our time to mourn is merely a stage of our growth, not a time of punishment or testing. We are never alone in this painful stage of growth. It is a holy time for us, a time to listen to God's whisper and remember his promises to us.

> *Walk with me each morning, Lord. May I bless the sunrise for the hope it brings of a new day. Be with me in the evening, Lord, that I may give thanks for the sunset, knowing that the darkness is only for a while.*

Difficulties are meant to rouse, not discourage. The human spirit is to grow strong by conflict.

—WILLIAM E. CHANNING

My husband gave me a beautiful diamond ring for my birthday a few years ago. Sometimes when I'm killing time, I'll sit and turn the diamond over in my hand, looking at it from different angles, watching the light reflect off its various facets.

How like a diamond we are as a result of our suffering. The diamond on my finger was nothing more than a lump of coal many eons ago. Yet as the weight of the world literally bore down on it, this black lump began to change. It wasn't crushed into nothingness or obliterated by the oppressive weight of the world upon its tiny self. Instead this rock began to change and harden, and eventually it emerged as a most precious gem, stronger and more beautiful than it ever could have been if it had remained a piece of black coal. As a diamond, the light is attracted to it, it sparkles and reflects the light back into the world, and it is seen by all as a thing of beauty. The diamond is stronger than all other gems and more valuable than gold.

In our suffering we are transformed, just as the diamond, into beautiful light-giving beings. We would not be so had suffering not tempered us thus.

> *Lord, take my sorrow and use it to mold and shape me into a better and more compassionate person than I was before. May the sufferings I endure temper my spirit and may I reflect light into the world just as a diamond does after its many years of change.*

. . . He was getting rather stupid—one of the chief signs of which was that he believed less and less in things he had never seen.

—George MacDonald

The more I try to learn about life the more I realize how ignorant I really am. There are so many mysteries and wonders in our universe. I doubt that any mortal being has ever unlocked all the mysteries before us. But in order to reach a state of enlightenment and higher knowledge, we need to continue the quest for understanding and knowledge throughout our lifetime. We must do so with a sense of wonder and open-mindedness. We must seek answers with the understanding that there are unbelievable miracles waiting to happen, uncounted discoveries to be made, amazing puzzles to be solved, and unending mysteries in our universe. The more we become aware of all that is before us, around us, and within us, the more we must come to be awestruck at the presence of God in all things.

God of all creation, may I be continually amazed and delighted in the great mysteries of this gift of life. I give thanks to you for the awesome and powerful wonders of this universe which you have shared with us, your most precious creation.

We cannot go to heaven on beds of down.
—RICHARD BRAITHEWAITE, *THE ENGLISH GENTLEMEN*, 1631

The sorrows that we endure in this life strengthen us. They make us more compassionate toward others. They help us to appreciate the good things that happen to us, and they often help to improve our perspective in life. Trivial incidents lose the power they once had to annoy us. Often as a result of suffering we become more spiritual people. We have reason to believe and to hope that there will be a better life after this one, and we become searchers for truths to bear this out. We learn to appreciate our loved ones more deeply, and we become more gentle and more patient than we were before.

Suffering, then, can be considered a gift of sorts. As a result of the adversities we endure, we are forced to grow, to learn, and to love more fully. Without the experience of sorrow in our lives, our growth might not be as meaningful. And, in the end, growth is the reason for our life here on earth: we are here to grow in knowledge, love, and faith. As we grow, therefore, we move closer to God who will one day call us home.

Lord, we cannot ask for lives free of pain or sorrow. But grant us the strength to endure the sufferings that

we meet in this life. May our trials
serve to strengthen us in love and faith.
May they bring us ever closer to you.

Physical strength is measured by what we can
carry; spiritual by what we can bear.

—SOURCE UNKNOWN

Before Andy died, I was quite convinced that the worst
thing that could possibly happen to me would be to
experience the death of one of my children. During those
first hours after Andy's death, when I realized that my
worst and darkest nightmares were coming to pass, I cried
out over and over again, "I won't survive this!" Indeed, I
had lost any desire to survive at all. The pain of losing my
son was much deeper than anything I had imagined, even
in my worst nightmares. I knew that hell itself could hold
no greater horrors for me than what I was experiencing.

Yet here I sit a few years later. Not only have I survived
the pain of Andy's death, I have emerged from it with a
new and stronger spiritual vision. I've faced my greatest
fear, I've suffered what I presume will be the greatest loss
of my life, and I have grown stronger.

Is there still the pain of losing him? Every day it's
there, although it rests more in the background of my
mind than it did months ago. Do I miss him? I ache with
the missing of him, and suppose I always will. Do I know
anything about death that I didn't know two years ago?
I've learned that, in spite of the pain I often feel, in spite
of the aching loss I experience from time to time, death
has not separated me from my child. He is still a vital part
of my life. And in reaching out for my son in the spiritual
world he now and forever inhabits, I have learned that I
too am a spiritual being, now and for all time. And when,

with my spiritual arms I reach out for help when the day's
burdens weigh me down, I fall into the arms of God.

> *Lord, let me never forget that I was*
> *created in your image. I am a spiri-*
> *tual being as well as a physical being.*
> *When I reach out for you, you give me*
> *the strength I need to carry the bur-*
> *dens I have chosen in this life on earth.*
> *Never let me forget that you are beside*
> *me and that you alone give me the*
> *strength I need for the day's journey.*

> Innocent questions make me wince. "Will the
> family all be home for Christmas? What are
> your children doing now. . . . How many chil-
> dren do you have?"
>
> —NICHOLAS WOLTERSTORFF, *LAMENT FOR A SON*

There will always be a sense of incompleteness in the
families of those who have lost a loved one. Family
pictures are difficult, knowing that there will always be one
person missing from the picture, no matter how many new
members are added to the family. Holidays are often bit-
tersweet with memories of other celebrations. I will never
be comfortable answering the question of how many children I have. In my mind and heart, I will always have four
children, but I don't always feel like explaining to strangers
that one of my children now calls heaven his home.

I remember one of my cousins taping a recording of
my grandmother singing "I'll Be Home for Christmas" in
her wonderfully throaty Sophie Tucker voice. Although we
didn't know it, that year was to be her last Christmas. She
died in May of the following year. Several months after her

death, this cousin was visiting my mother's house and offered to play the recording for us. None of us was ready to hear our dear grandmother's voice. It would have been too painful at the time. But ever since, when I hear that song on the radio, it never fails to evoke sweet memories of my fiery-tempered Irish grandmother.

Our lives change with each loved one's passing. Nothing is ever the same again. We do move on. We welcome new members into our families and we make new memories. But the love and the memories and the special place in our hearts for those who are gone stays with us until we meet them again.

> *Lord, we will always hold close to our hearts our love of those who have died. They will always be a part of our lives and our history. Keep them close to you, and may they enjoy all the rewards of heaven. May they always be aware of the love we have for them, and may they also look forward to the day of our reunion.*

Just after Robbie died, the idea of living for any appreciable length of time was horrifying. All I could envision was an endless number of days and hours stretching into infinity and all filled with pain and grief. . . . Now I find myself and my family going and doing and functioning and taking a joy in life and its challenges. I never believed this was possible. But I assure you it is true.

—HARRIET S. SCHIFF, *THE BEREAVED PARENT*

In this sad world of ours, sorrow comes to all, and it often comes with bitter agony. Perfect relief is not possible, except with time. You cannot now believe that you will ever feel better. But this is not true. You are sure to be happy again. Knowing this, truly believing it, will make you less miserable now. I have had enough experience to make this statement.

—ABRAHAM LINCOLN

A colleague once asked me if the pain and turmoil he was experiencing ever ceased. Much later in life, when he had been through the darkness, he told me: "The one thing that I kept clinging to and which gave me hope was when you answered my question 'Does it get better?' with 'Yes it does. It may take a while but it does get better.'"

—JOYCE RUPP, *LITTLE PIECES OF LIGHT*

Among the many people who stopped by our house on the day Andy died was a young man named Shawn, a friend of my son Sean. When our boys were on the junior varsity football team their sophomore year in high school, Shawn's mother collapsed and died at a football game one evening. It was a terrible tragedy and one that affected Shawn's family and friends very deeply. I don't remember what anyone said to me the afternoon of Andy's death, except Shawn. I remember this big kid lumbering up the stairs of our front porch as I met him at the door. He wrapped his arms around me and whispered, "It gets easier."

Those words were the strongest medicine I could have received. The one thing I most needed to hear in the days after Andy's death were assurances that I would not always feel this intense pain. I doubted that I could survive such a great grief and at the same time worried that I would survive it and go on living with this horrible hurt. I didn't care

219

at the time that Andy was in a better place, free of pain. I wasn't interested in God's will or any of the ineffective offerings other people were making, trying to help me feel better. All I wanted to know was that this horrifying, searing pain wasn't going to last forever. And the only one who could assure me of that was one who had been through this before. I didn't want to talk to anyone who would tell me that I would never get over this, because I was convinced that a pain this overwhelming would literally kill me. A part of me welcomed the idea of death as an escape from the pain.

But it does get easier. Eventually, gradually, I began to realize that life does resume some semblance of normalcy. I found myself slowly having more good days than bad ones, and when the pangs of sadness struck, as they occasionally did, they didn't fill me with a sense of panic. I knew that the sad feelings wouldn't last forever, and that life could again be enjoyed. Those of us who have been along this road can perform no greater kindness for the newly bereaved than to assure them of this truth.

Father, you give me the strength I need to look forward to my future with hope and confidence. I know that there will be times when I will stumble on this journey, but you will always be beside me to set me right and remind me that I will never be alone. I thank you for the moments of laughter I find in my life, and I cling to you in moments of sorrow. You are always beside me.

Resources and Recommended Readings

Beattie, Melody. *The Language of Letting Go*. New York: MJF Books, 1990.

Bernardin, Joseph Cardinal. *The Gift of Peace*. Chicago: Loyola Press, 1997.

Bernstein, Judith R., Ph.D. *When the Bough Breaks: Forever After the Death of a Son or Daughter*. Kansas City, MO: Andrews McMeel, 1997.

Cahill, Thomas. *The Gifts of the Jews: How a Tribe of Desert Nomads Changed the Way Everyone Thinks and Feels*. New York: Nan A. Talese, 1998.

Chittister, Joan. *There Is a Season*. New York: Orbis Books, 1996.

Cox-Chapman, Mally. *The Case for Heaven*. New York: Putnam, 1995.

D'Arcy, Paula. *Gift of the Red Bird*. New York: Crossroad, 1996.

Davison, Rebecca and Susan Mesner, eds. *The Treasury of Religious and Spiritual Quotations: Words to Live By*. Pleasantville, NY: Reader's Digest, 1994.

Devers, Edie. *Goodbye Again: Experiences With Departed Loved Ones*. Kansas City, MO: Andrews McMeel, 1997.

Dobson, James. *When God Doesn't Make Sense*. Wheaton, IL: Tyndale House, 1993.

Dyer, Wayne W. *Wisdom of the Ages*. New York: HarperCollins, 1998.

Elliott, William. *Tying Rocks to Clouds: Meetings and Conversations with Wise and Spiritual People*. New York: Doubleday, 1996.

Finkbeiner, Ann K. *After the Death of a Child: Living With Loss Through the Years*. New York: Free Press, 1995.

Gibran, Kahlil. *The Prophet*. New York: Alfred A. Knopf, 1999.

Guggenheim, Bill and Judy Guggenheim. *Hello From Heaven!* New York: Bantam Books, 1995.

Harvey, Nicholas Peter. *Death's Gift: Chapters on Resurrection and Bereavement*. Grand Rapids, MI: Eerdmans, 1995.

Komp, Diane M. *A Window to Heaven: When Children See Life in Death*. Grand Rapids, MI: Zondervan, 1992.

Kushner, Harold S. *When Bad Things Happen to Good People*. New York: Avon Books, 1981.

Lewis, C. S. *A Grief Observed*. London: Faber & Faber, 1961.

Livingston, Gordon. *Only Spring: On Mourning the Death of My Son*. New York: HarperCollins, 1995.

Lucado, Max. *The Gift for All People: Thoughts on God's Great Grace.* Sisters, OR: Multnomah Publishers, 1999.

————. *God Came Near.* Sisters, OR: Multnomah Publishers, 1987.

McCracken, Anne and Mary Semel. *A Broken Heart Still Beats: After Your Child Dies.* Center City, MN: Hazeldon, 1998.

Mehren, Elizabeth. *After the Darkest Hour the Sun Will Shine Again.* New York: Simon & Schuster, 1997.

Moore, Thomas. *Care of the Soul.* New York: Harper Perennial, 1992.

Prabhavananda, Swami and Christopher Isherwood, trans. *Bhagavad-Gita.* New York: Barnes and Noble, 1994.

Rupp, Joyce. *The Cup of Our Life: A Guide for Spiritual Growth.* Notre Dame, IN: Ave Maria Press, 1997.

————. *Little Pieces of Light: Darkness and Personal Growth.* Mahwah, NJ: Paulist Press, 1994.

————. *Praying Our Goodbyes.* Notre Dame, IN: Ave Maria Press, 1995.

Schiff, Harriet. *The Bereaved Parent.* New York: Penguin, 1977.

Sittser, Gerald L. *A Grace Disguised: How the Soul Grows Through Loss.* Grand Rapids, MI: Zondervan, 1996.

Tada, Joni Eareckson. *Heaven: Your Real Home.* Grand Rapids, MI: Zondervan, 1995.

Theroux, Phyllis, ed. *The Book of Eulogies: A Collection of Memorial Tributes, Poetry, Essays, and Letters of Condolence.* New York: Scribner, 1997.

Verploegh, Harry. *3,000 Quotations from the Writings of George MacDonald.* Grand Rapids, MI: Fleming H. Revell, 1996.

Williamson, Marianne. *Illuminata: A Return to Prayer.* New York: Berkley, 1994.

Wolterstorff, Nicholas. *Lament for a Son.* Grand Rapids, MI: Eerdmans, 1987.

Ziglar, Zig. *Confessions of a Grieving Christian.* Nashville, TN: Thomas Nelson, 1998.

Ann Dawson lives in Forsyth, Illinois, and is a regular contributor to the column "Prairie Talk" in her local newspaper. If you would like to contact Ann, she can be reached by e-mail at AKDawson7@aol.com.